TRANSLATION STUDIES

WITHDRAWN

TRANSLATION STUDIES
AN INTEGRATED APPROACH

MARY SNELL-HORNBY

Revised Edition

JOHN BENJAMINS PUBLISHING COMPANY
AMSTERDAM/PHILADELPHIA

1988/1995

Revised edition, 1995

Library of Congress Cataloging-in-Publication Data

Snell-Hornby, Mary.
    Translation studies.
Bibliography: p.
1. Translating and interpreting. I. Title.
P306.S58   1988   418'.02   88-7606
ISBN 90 272 2060 3 (Eur.)/1-55619-052-2 (US)(pb; alk. paper)

John Benjamins Publishing Co. • P.O.Box 75577 • 1070 AN Amsterdam • The Netherlands
John Benjamins North America • P.O.Box 27519 • Philadelphia PA 19118-0519 • USA

Table of contents

Preface to the Revised Edition

When this book appeared on the market seven years ago, the author would never have believed it could achieve the circulation figures to merit a Revised Edition. The study started out modestly as an academic thesis presenting an approach — by definition a tentative word — and its topic still seemed then to be of marginal interest in the world of scholarship. Fortunately however the publication coincided with the breathtaking development of Translation Studies as an independent discipline, and the ideas offered here were able to make a contribution to a meanwhile prolific international discussion.

The revisions consist mainly in making the German quotations transparent for an English-speaking readership — either by translation or paraphrase. I have also added a comment on my "tentative prognosis" of 1987 on the future of Translation Studies — from the perspective of 1995. Some additions have been made to the Bibliography, but these were by necessity selective: to do justice to the wealth of publications that have appeared over the last few years, one would have to write a new book. And finally, an index of names and key terms has been added for easier reference — my thanks are due to Gudrun Huemer for compiling it.

I would like to thank the many colleagues who have made comments and suggestions for this edition, whether informally or in the form of reviews — these were where possible taken into consideration. And my sincere thanks go to John Benjamins Publishers, in particular to Bertie Kaal, for years of efficient and friendly cooperation.

Vienna, January 1995   Mary Snell-Hornby

Preface to the First Edition

"Sprachwissenschaftlich orientierte Übersetzungsstudien können also kein grundsätzliches und theoretisches Angebot für die Erforschung der literarischen Übersetzung zur Verfügung stellen." This statement was made in 1984 by scholars working on a long-term interdisciplinary project devoted to literary translation at the University of Göttingen.[1] For the past nine months the author of the present study has had the pleasure of working as visiting linguist with those same scholars and persuading them that their statement needs at least some modification. It is certainly true that the relationship of linguistics to translation studies, especially to literary translation, is complicated, that only a limited number of issues in linguistics are relevant for translation and that linguistic models can hardly ever be adopted wholesale. There are however approaches and methods originating in linguistics which have been successfully adapted for translation, and there are concepts developed from the study of language which have considerable potential even for literary translation. Some such approaches, concepts and methods are presented in this study, in the hope of bridging the gap between literary translation and linguistics. The conclusions are based on work done mainly in English and German, but the main principles, as the work in Göttingen has confirmed, should apply to some extent to any language-pair.

The author has an honours degree in German Language and Literature, one research degree in German Literature and another in English Linguistics. She has worked as a translator in various fields (mainly from German and French into English) and has taught translation at university level to students of English and to trainee translators; she has also lectured in translation theory in various European universities. Some results of the practical work in translation were published in her two books *German Thought in English Idiom. Exercises in Translation and Style for Final Year Students* (München: Hueber 1967, [3]1977) and *German-English Prose Translation* (München: Hueber, 1972, [2]1978). What is presented here is an integrated concept based on the combined experience in the theory and practice of translation, in the

hope that it will make some contribution to the development of this exciting
new discipline.

Meilen, May 1987   Mary Snell-Hornby

Note

1.   Sonderforschungsbereich 309, "Die Literarische Übersetzung", Hauptantrag an die
      Deutsche Forschungsgemeinschaft, 1984, p.16.

0. Introduction

> In translation the dialectic of unison and plurality is dramatically at work. In one sense, each act of translation is an endeavour to abolish multiplicity and to bring different world-pictures back into perfect congruence. In another sense, it is an attempt to reinvent the shape of meaning, to find and justify an alternate statement. The craft of the translator is (...) deeply ambivalent: it is exercised in a radical tension between impulses to facsimile and impulses to appropriate recreation. (Steiner 1975: 235)

George Steiner's monumental book *After Babel. Aspects of Language and Translation* deals primarily with the translation of great works of art. The "radical tension" between reproduction and recreation with the "dialectic of unison and plurality" is not however only limited to literary translation, but is — to a greater or lesser extent — the essence of any translator's dilemma.

For two thousand years translation theory (some call it "traditional," others now dismiss it as "prescientific") was concerned only with outstanding works of art. For the last forty years "translation science," or translatology, has been trying to establish itself as a new discipline focussing on an undefined and idealized "common core" of general language, but with concepts that in effect apply only to technical terminology. Literary language was excluded as being "deviant," inaccessible to scientific analysis.

This study is an attempt to bridge the gap. It is not (as the reader familiar with recent developments in translation theory might possibly infer from the title) a study on literary translation; it is rather an attempt to present recently developed concepts and methods, both from translation theory and linguistics, in such a way that they could be usefully employed in the theory, practice and analysis of literary translation.

This presupposes some radical changes in thinking: firstly, in conceptualization and categorization, and secondly in the approach to translation itself. The age-old polarized dichotomy (such as word vs. sense, which dominated traditional translation theory ever since Cicero) and the classical box-like category of objectivist and reductionist tradition (such as neatly delimited text-types and rigid equivalence-types, which paralyzed the development of the linguistically oriented translatology) have been replaced by a holistic, gestalt-like principle based on prototypes dynamically focussed at points on a cline (cf. p. 32 and p. 89). In this way, the multi-dimensional character of language with its dynamic tension of paradoxes and seemingly conflicting forces becomes the basis for translation. Secondly, the idea must be abandoned that translation is merely a matter of isolated words, an *idée fixe* that characterized work on translation until quite recently: in our concept translation begins with the text-in-situation as an integral part of the cultural background, whereby text-analysis proceeds from the macro-structure of the text to the micro-unit of the word, this being seen, not as an isolatable item, but in its relevance and function within the text. Furthermore, the text cannot be considered as a static specimen of language (an idea still dominant in practical translation classes), but essentially as the verbalized expression of an author's intention as understood by the translator as reader, who then recreates this whole for another readership in another culture. This dynamic process explains why new translations of literary works are constantly in demand, and why *the* perfect translation does not exist.

The demand that translation studies should be viewed as an independent discipline — an idea that goes back to Nida's work in the 1960's — has come from several quarters in recent years, from such academically-minded translation scholars as Susan Bassnett-McGuire (*Translation Studies*, 1980/Revised Edition 1991) to practitioners such as Hartmut Lange ("Begegnung zwischen Praxis und Lehre. Ein BDÜ Symposium," *MDÜ* 1984/1). Up to now however no substantial attempt has been made to specify the content of such an independent discipline which would include both literary and special language translation.[1] This study is intended as a step in that direction. In other words, it is essentially a study in the theory and practice of translation; it can only indirectly be assigned to the field of literary studies in that it is concerned with literary translation, and it is not intended to be a contribution to the discipline of linguistics. As will emerge during the course of the following chapters, translation studies, as a culturally oriented subject, draws on a number of disciplines, including psychology (1.3), ethnology (2.1) and philosophy (2.1), without being a subdivision of any of them. Similarly, it can and should utilize relevant concepts and methods developed from the study of language (this despite massive misgivings on the part of scholars in literary translation, cf. 1.2.4 below) without automatically becoming a branch of linguistics or having to adopt linguistic methods and theoretical constructs wholesale. Linguistics is concerned with the theory and description of language for its own sake, translation studies with the theory and description of recreating concrete texts, whether literary, specialized or general. What is therefore important for translation studies in the *usability* of the method, the *potential* within a concept, and this must be both broad enough to have general validity and flexible enough to be adapted to the individual — and often idiosyncratic — text. As by no means all linguistic concepts and methods are relevant to translation, it is clear that — as with any interdisciplinary work — a specific selection must be made. This is not however identical with haphazard eclecticism, and it means that work in the field of translation cannot aim at following the course of discussions within the discipline of linguistics where these have no direct bearing on translation theory or practice. Presupposing such limitations therefore, this study presents some concepts and methods from linguistics which have shown themselves to be relevant for translation, and they are here further developed for use in translations studies.

Chapter I presents a conception of text, language and categorization as the basis for an independent, integrated discipline of translation studies embracing the whole spectrum of language, whether literary, "ordinary" or "general" language, or language for special purposes. First, the approach to be adopted here is situated against the conceptual background of both traditional and modern translation theory, and a detailed explanation is given of why the concept of equivalence — as a term, as a notion and in its innumerable different usages — is an unsuitable basis for an integrated theory of translation. The principle of the gestalt and the concept of the prototypology are then presented as alternatives to traditional forms of categorization, and they are exemplified in an integrated theoretical model which relates textual prototypes to those criteria relevant for them in translation.

Chapter 2 presents the notion of translation, not as a mere transcoding process as in linguistically oriented translatology, but as a cross-cultural event. Recent translation theories based on this view are discussed (2.2) and some new ideas and concepts are put forward: language — not as a Saussurean dichotomy of *langue* and *parole* — but as a spectrum of system, norm and text, whereby the three prototypical concepts interact in a constant dynamic tension. This is then illustrated on the basis of language *dimension* and cultural *perspective* in literary translation — with examples from Stoppard and Lewis Carroll — and special attention is paid to the problem of translating metaphor (with an example from Thomas Mann).

In Chapter 3 some theories and concepts from linguistics are presented, and illustrated by examples, in their potential relevance for translation. First, a macro-level analysis is demonstrated on the basis of a brief sketch by Somerset Maugham, whereby the concept of *field progression* has been developed from text-linguistics (Greimas' concept of the *isotope* and Stolze's method of analyzing semantic fields in the text). In 3.3 Fillmore's scenes-and-frames semantics is discussed as a basis for the understanding and recreation of the text by the translator, whereby the linguistic *frame* interacts with the experiential *scene* behind the text. In 3.4 the speech act theory of Austin and Searle is applied in a contrastive model showing structural differences in German and English public directives, and finally, the dynamic adjective (3.5), in an extended semantic definition, is analyzed as a basic source of difficulty for the translator. Here the tension between norm and text becomes especially clear, and the analysis serves as a basis for reconsidering the traditional methods of bilingual lexicography; the chapter closes with a discussion of the varying interlingual relationships as an alternative to the often misleading dictionary equivalent.

Chapter 4 takes a broad view at the spectrum of text-types from special to literary language, in their relevance for translation. A closer look at the situation of the source text and the function of the translation (cf. 2.2) shows that the status of the literary source text is higher than with most other text-types. Similarly, the factor of style — as individual choice versus group convention — is more decisive in literary translation than with special or general language. By way of conclusion, Chapter 5 takes a look at the future and offers a tentative prognosis for translation studies as an independent discipline from the viewpoints of 1987 and 1995.

As far as possible, the concepts presented here are illustrated by examples, some literary (Tom Stoppard, Thomas Mann, Lawrence Durrell, Dylan Thomas), others are extracts from newspaper articles to illustrate phenomena common to both literary and general language. Three of the four texts discussed in Chapter 4 are from the author's own workshop; they are presented, not as "model translations" in the global sense (a concept rejected by modern translation theory) but as concrete assignments serving a specific function within a given situation.

At present, translation is a topic which anyone and everyone professes to know about and a craft which many laymen with a smattering of foreign languages think they can master. This study is a contribution to those many efforts now being made to rouse awareness for what most professional translators know their metier to be: a skill demanding utmost proficiency, specialized knowledge and the sensitivity of an artist, which — like other activities of its kind — should be left to the expert.

Note

1. Even the pioneering work of James S. Holmes (1988:65 ff.) concentrated on literary translation. Meanwhile however much work has been done in this direction (cf. the collection of papers in Snell-Hornby, Pöchhacker and Kaindl 1994).

1. Translation studies as an independent discipline

1.1 Translation and traditional language study

The study of foreign languages and literatures is firmly anchored in the Western university tradition. Perspective and focus vary from one country to another, but the basic pattern is recognizable almost everywhere: each department concentrates on one foreign language and the literature written in it (this is typical of the British system and where English is studied as a foreign language) or on a group of languages and their respective literatures, such as the Romance or Slavonic languages (this being typical of Continental universities and to some extent of those in North America).[1] Traditionally, such departments have developed independently of each other and are themselves divided into two clear sections, one concerned with the study of literature and the other with the study of language. In recent years, university reform and the foundation of new universities have in some countries led to a reshuffling of the traditional departments, resulting on the one hand in Language Centres and on the other in Institutes of Comparative Literature;[2] in this way the compartmentalization of the various language subjects has been overcome, but the rift between the study of language and the study of literature has been deepened.

It is this rift that has always characterized the theory of translation and even today still dominates translation studies. In practice of course texts of all kinds have been translated since the scribal activities of Old Babylonia over three thousand years ago,[3] but translation theory was limited until quite recently to cultural monuments such as the Bible or the works of Classical Antiquity, as well as outstanding works of literature, particularly poetry and drama. Translated texts from everyday life were studied, if at all, merely as specimens of language at a given stage of development,[4] and traditional philology did not concern itself with translation theory.

During the course of the last thirty years however, the study of language has undergone radical changes: the focus of interest has widened from the purely historical to the contemporary, from the prescriptive to the descriptive, from the theoretical system to the concrete realization, from the micro-level of the sign to the macro-structure of the text. The combined impact of these developments facilitated the emergence of a linguistically oriented translation theory, which, particularly in Germany — with the integration of translator training institutes into the universities — established itself as the new academic subject of *Übersetzungswissenschaft*, or translatology.

The status of the new discipline is however still uncertain, and in the traditional language departments it is at best known from hearsay. Even the historically oriented theories of literary translation remain exotic material, rarely taught and virtually unknown. For most students of foreign languages, the subject of translation is limited to "practical" translation exercises, a relic from the heyday of Latin classes in schools and now a highly disputed method of foreign language teaching,[5] whereby a text — or rather a text fragment — has to be rendered sentence by sentence and phrase by phrase in the foreign language. With this background it is hardly surprising that translation has such low status and translation theory is viewed with such scepticism in academic circles.

The starting point of our study therefore represents the very opposite of our ultimate aim. At present the subject of translation, especially as it is seen in the traditional language departments, is fragmented and disconnected: the different languages are taught in separate departments, literature and language are represented by different professors, translation theory, whether literary or linguistic, is barely known, and translation practice is relegated entirely to the low-level status of practical language teaching.

1.2 Literary and linguistic orientations

Traditional translation theory has been intensively investigated, and it is not the aim of this study to go into it in detail. Störig (1973) provides a cross-section of the main contributions from St Jerome to the present day, including those of Luther, Goethe, Schleiermacher, Buber and Benjamin. Of the diverse historical reviews of translation and translation theory, Mounin (1967) remains a classic with one of the first connecting links to modern theory, while Kelly (1979) presents a broad survey, interweaving various linguistic approaches. For the most part, such well-trodden ground

lies outside the field of the present study: the aim of the following historical outline is rather to trace the underlying concepts of and attitudes
towards translation through the relevant periods of its development.

1.2.1 The dichotomy of word and sense

By far the most influential concept in the history of translation is that
age-old dichotomy of word and sense, which traditional translation theory
never managed to overcome, and which still besets translation studies
today.

It was Cicero in the first century BC who departed from the dogma
that translation necessarily consisted of a word-for-word rendering and who
so eloquently formulated the alternative: "Non ut interpres ... sed ut
orator" (Mounin 1967:24). For the next two thousand years translation
theory was mainly limited to a heated discussion of this dichotomy, the
pendulum of current opinion swinging from one side to the other. In Bible
translation, with the deep-seated belief in the sacred Word of God, the
absolute criterion was the literal word of the original, and this explains
Jerome's defensive attitude when he declares in his letter (57) to Pam-
machius that when translating from Greek (with the exception of the Holy
Scriptures) he does not translate word for word but "sense for sense", thus
consciously opposing the dogma of the time:

> Ego enim non solum fateor, sed libera voce profiteor me in interpretatione
> Graecorum absque scripturis sanctis, ubi et verborum ordo misterium est,
> *non verbum e verbo sed sensum exprimere de sensu.*
> (1980:13, emphasis added)

Well over a thousand years later, in 1530, Luther was to fight a similar bat-
tle with the Church authorities of his time over the translation of the Bible
into German. He defended the same basic principle as Jerome, but his
words were a good deal more aggressive, as emerges from the celebrated
passage in his *Sendbrief vom Dolmetschen*:

> We shouldn't go and ask the Latin text how to speak German, as those
> fools do, we must ask the housewives and children, the ordinary man in
> the street and listen to what they say and translate accordingly — then
> they'll understand and see we're talking proper German to them.
> (cit. Störig 1973:21, my translation)

The debate over the varying merits of the "faithful" and the "free" —
the latter culminating in the "belles infidèles," or the free adaptations

popular in France — continued to rage in Europe (Mounin 1967: 42ff.), and it found eloquent expression in Germany during the early years of the 19th century, when translation blossomed again with the Romantic movement. On 24 June 1813 Schleiermacher read his much-quoted treatise "Ueber die verschiedenen Methoden des Uebersezens" (On the different methods of translating) to the Royal Academy of Sciences in Berlin, culminating in the maxim:

> Either the translator leaves the author in peace and moves the reader towards him, or he leaves the reader in peace and adapts the author. The two methods are so completely different that the one chosen must be followed as consistently as possible, as a mixture can have most unsatisfactory results, whereby author and reader completely lose sight of each other.
>
> (cit. Störig 1973:47, my translation)

The emphasis has shifted now from the categoric "not ... but" to the more tolerant alternative "either ... or," but the rigid dichotomy remains, and Schleiermacher makes it clear in his treatise that he favours the method of *Verfremdung*, or translation that is "faithful" to the original. As the contributions in Störig's anthology show, the debate continued well into the 20th century, the most extreme case being presented by Benjamin (1923), who returns to the concept of the "heiliger Text" and declares that the interlinear version of the Bible is the ideal of all translation (Störig 1973:169). In southern Europe equally drastic conclusions were drawn, by Croce (1902) and by Ortega y Gasset (1973), who maintained that ultimately translation is an "impossible undertaking."[6] Despite such admissions of resignation and despair however, it still remains an indisputable fact that translation has been going on, and much of it successfully, throughout European civilization. What was wrong was rather the nature of the theory itself with its onesided and absolute demands, as well as the limitations imposed by the material. Both the Bible and the great works of Classical Antiquity rather represent special cases of translation than a broad basis on which to build a theory of general validity — and such a theory was hindered by a deliberate and artificial reduction of the field of study. Another clear-cut dichotomy established by Schleiermacher in the same treatise — and still upheld in translation studies today — was that between "das eigentliche Uebersezen" (translation proper) and his conception of "mere interpreting" ("das bloße Dolmetschen"), meaning, not the specialized activity of conference interpreting as it is understood today, but the translation, both written and oral, of everyday texts on matters of business, law and administration, which were for him mundane and mechanical matters unworthy of scholarly attention. His "Uebersezen" applied only to literary works of art, and his theoretical framework was hence limited to only one section of what is now understood as translation.

1.2.2 *Categories and principles*

Apart from the polarized approach represented in the dichotomy as described above, traditional translation theory also presented means of differentiating and categorizing translation types. This approach was the one adopted by Dryden (1680) in his *Preface to Ovid's Epistles, Translated by Several Hands*. Here he distinguishes between *metaphrase*, or word-for-word translation, and its opposite, *imitation*, which is confined by neither word nor sense but represents a loose approximation of an author's emotions or passion; between these two extremes is *paraphrase*, which expresses the thought or sense of the original without being enslaved by the words. Dryden makes it quite clear where his preferences lie. For him the least desirable type of translation is metaphrase, which he compares to "dancing on ropes with fettered legs" (cit. Watson 1962:269), and he declares bluntly:

> 'Tis almost impossible to translate verbally, and well, at the same time (...). In short, the verbal copier is encumbered with so many difficulties at once that he can never disentangle himself from all. He is to consider at the same time the thought of his author, and his words, and to find out the counterpart to each in another language; and, besides this, he is to confine himself to the compass of numbers, and the slavery of rhyme.
>
> (cit. Watson 1962:269)

Imitation, on the other hand, is described as "the most advantageous way for a translator to shew himself, but the greatest wrong which can be done to the memory and reputation of the dead" (cit. Watson 1962:271). In other words, both literal translation and imitation are "the two extremes which ought to be avoided" (cit. Watson 1962:271). However, Dryden does soften this severely prescriptive attitude by admitting that the type of translation should vary with the author concerned: so "wild and ungovernable a poet" as Pindar can only be rendered in English by way of imitation (as in Cowley's translation), whereas "regular, intelligible authors" like Virgil and Ovid do not justify excessive liberties in a translation (cit. Watson 1962:271). Ironically, Dryden admits at the end of his *Preface* that in his own translations he himself has "transgressed the rules which I have given,

and taken more liberty than a just translation will allow" (cit. Watson
1962:273), implying that in practice a translator tends to allow himself more
scope for free expression in his work than the theoretician or the critic
would strictly permit.

Dryden's theoretical concept is therefore not a symmetrical trichotomy,
but a flexible system of categories: between the two less desirable extremes
is a recommended "golden mean" to be varied according to the needs
of the author — or work — to be translated. Having explained his objec-
tions to the slavishly literal translation on the one hand and the overly
loose imitation on the other, Dryden concludes his argument by presenting
some basic principles and prerequisites for a good translation. For the
translation theorist of the late 20th century — even one who has read none
of Dryden's works — they sound strangely familiar. The four basic tenets
are these:

(1)   No man is capable of translating poetry who, besides a genius to
      that art, is not a master both of his author's language and of his
      own.

(2)   Nor must we understand the language only of the poet, but his
      particular turn of thoughts and of expression, which are the
      characters that distinguish and, as it were, individuate him from
      all other writers. (...)

(3)   The like care must be taken of the more outward ornaments, the
      words.

(4)   The sense of an author, generally speaking, is to be sacred and
      inviolable.

                                              (cit. Watson 1962: 271f.)

Principles and rules of this kind have surfaced from time to time during the
course of the past centuries, and Dryden was not even the first theorist to
formulate them. We find similar views expressed in 1540 by the French
scholar Etienne Dolet in a miniature treatise of only four pages entitled "La
manière de bien traduire d'une langue en autre" (How to achieve a good
translation from one language into another) (Cary 1963), which presents
the following five basic guidelines:

(1) the translator must have a perfect understanding of his author's
     message and material,

(2) he should have complete mastery of both source and target language,

(3) he should not translate word for word,

(4) he should beware of Latinisms and use idiomatic language,

(5) he should strive after a smooth, elegant, unpretentious and even style.

Very similar views were to be expressed in 1790 by Alexander Tytler in a series of lectures delivered to the Royal Society and published the following year as the celebrated *Essay on the Principles of Translation*. This is based on three "laws of translation" which Tytler formulates as follows (1978:16):

It will follow,

I. That the Translation should give a complete transcript of the ideas of the original work.

II. That the style and manner of writing should be of the same character with that of the original.

III. That the translation should have all the ease of the original composition.

In explaining the first of these general rules, the author emphasizes that "it is indispensably necessary, that he (the translator) should have a perfect knowledge of the original, and a competent acquaintance with the subject of which it treats." (1978:17) Though critical of the excessive licence he sees in Dryden's translations (1978:47, 97ff., 123ff.), Tytler acknowledges his debt to Dryden's theoretical writing, especially the close of the *Preface* with the basic principles of translation, which he quotes in full (1978:247ff.), so we may safely assume that the similarity of their ideas was not accidental, but no mention is made in the *Essay* to Etienne Dolet. Whether Dolet was known to Tytler or not, it is interesting that all three theorists arived at virtually the same basic conclusions, not only by studying the Classical works of art in translation, but also through personal experience as translators.

1.2.3 *The illusion of equivalence*

It is significant that all the "general rules" and "basic guidelines" quoted above implicitly refer to the entire phenomenon of translation. In making his distinction between metaphrase, paraphrase and imitation, Dryden even states quite openly: "All translation, I suppose, may be reduced to these three heads." (cit. Watson 1962:268) In actual fact however, he is thinking only of the translation of poetry. This phenomenon, whereby a theorist makes global observations on translation in general, but actually means only one, often narrow area of it, still characterizes translation studies today — to the detriment of a general theory of translation. Nowhere is this more evident than in the work of the two main schools of translation theory which now dominate the scene in Europe.

The first of these is represented by the subject of *Übersetzungswissenschaft* developed in Germany by the so-called Leipzig School (the main representatives being Otto Kade, Gert Jäger and Albrecht Neubert) and by scholars such as Wolfram Wilss, Katharina Reiss and Werner Koller in Western Germany. This branch of translation studies is linguistically oriented and was for a long time clearly defined as a subdiscipline of Applied Linguistics, whose aims and methods were unquestioningly adopted. Just as linguistics aims at making the study of language strictly scientific, *Übersetzungswissenschaft* aims at making the study of translation rigorously scientific and watertight; traditional translation theory was dismissed as *vorwissenschaftlich* (prescientific), "subjective" or even "naive." Like linguistics, *Übersetzungswissenschaft* adopted views and methods of the exact sciences, in particular mathematics and formal logic, and in both cases the view is now frequently expressed that such methods have led to a dead end. In the words of the Romanist and translation theorist Fritz Paepcke (personal communication): "Die Sprachwissenschaft ist eine Wissenschaft ohne Sprache" (The science of language is a science without language).

As a linguistically oriented branch of translation theory, translatology in its broad sense is not limited to the German *Übersetzungswissenschaft*. In the 1960s, during the boom of the strictly scientific linguistic theories, English-speaking linguists also developed theoretical approaches to translation. In the United States the most influential scholar was undoubtedly Eugene A. Nida (Nida 1964; Nida and Taber 1969), who, on the basis of his own rich experience in Bible translating, developed a theory of translation which included concepts from transformational grammar. In England, J.C. Catford (1965) based his translation theory on the systemic grammar concept of the British linguist M.A.K. Halliday. Twenty years later, Nida is still an influential figure, though primarily as a Bible translator rather than a theoretical linguist, while Catford's approach is now generally considered dated and of mere historical interest.[7]

What all the linguistically oriented schools of translation theory have in common however, is the central concept of translation equivalence (German *Äquivalenz*), which shifted the focus of translation theory away from the traditional dichotomy of "faithful" or "free" to a presupposed interlingual tertium comparationis. Wilss assesses the development as follows:

> A second problem is the notorious controversy on the right perspective of the translation process — literal or free translation, source-language oriented or target-language oriented translation. Only when it was realized how sterile this debate was and when the interlingual tertium comparationis was made the central point of reference in theoretical work on translation, did translatology begin to take on sharper contours. (1980:10, my translation)

In this function of relating to the envisaged interlingual tertium comparationis, the term *equivalence* or *equivalent* was for many years considered essential in any definition of translation. Catford writes as follows:

> Translation may be defined as follows: The replacement of textual material in one language (SL) by equivalent textual material in another language (TL). (1965:20)

and he even maintains:

> The central problem of translation practice is that of finding TL translation equivalents. A central task of translation theory is that of defining the nature and conditions of translation equivalence. (1965:21)

Right up to the end of the 1970s, definitions of translation can be described as variations on this central theme. In Nida and Taber we find:

> Translating consists in reproducing in the receptor language the closest natural equivalent of the source language message, first in terms of meaning and secondly in terms of style. (1969:12)

Ten years later in Germany we read: "Als Übersetzung im eigentlichen Sinne bezeichnen wir nur, was bestimmten *Äquivalenzforderungen normativer Art* genügt' (Koller 1979:79) (For us a translation in the real sense of the word must fulfil specific requirements of normative equivalence).

Though they originated over a period of fourteen years and against a background of three different schools of thought in translation theory, these definitions are all strikingly similar: while there are shifts in secondary focus (such as the distinction between "natural" and "normative," the differentiation between meaning and style or the varying emphasis on text or message), each definition is constructed round the central term *equivalence/Äquivalenz* (or a derivative), which itself however remains unspecified.

In the earlier stages of the discussion opinions varied as to what was to be equivalent, whether words or even segments of words or longer units. Gradually the concept of the *translation unit* emerged, which was generally understood as a cohesive segment lying between the level of the word and the sentence. Equivalence was then sought, depending on the views of the theorist, either between translation units (as in Kade 1968) or at the level of the entire text (as in Wilss' definition quoted above), or at both levels, as in the conception of Katharina Reiss (1971:11ff., my translation):

> In translation equivalence should be established both between the complete text of the original and the target-language version and between the individual translation units.

In the linguistically oriented views on translation theory up to the early 1970s the text was then seen as a linear sequence of units, and translation was merely a *transcoding* process involving the substitution of a sequence of equivalent units. This emerges clearly from Koller's definition of 1972:

> Linguistically translation can be described as transcoding or substitution: Elements a_1, a_2, a_3... of the language system L_1 are replaced by elements b_1, b_2, b_3 of the language system L_2. (1972:69f., my translation)

In this approach the translation process then consisted in determining the translation units and selecting the so-called "optimal equivalent" from the diverse "potential equivalents" provided by the target language (see Kade 1968; Reiss 1971; also Diller and Kornelius 1978). The sum total of target units would then render the interlingual tertium comparationis expressed in the source text.

The argumentation seems plausible, but it rests on a shaky basis: it presupposes a degree of symmetry between languages which makes the postulated equivalence possible. Nowhere is the fallacy in such thinking better illustrated than in the term *equivalence* itself. From the above selection of definitions one has the impression that the German term *Äquivalenz* and the English term *equivalence* are identical and themselves exemplify the linguistic relationship they set out to denote. To my knowledge no translation theorist has ever doubted that *Äquivalenz* and *equivalence* are perfectly symmetrical renderings of a common interlingual tertium comparationis. In fact the opposite is true: on closer investigation subtle but crucial differences emerge between the two terms, so that they should rather be considered as warning examples of the treacherous *illusion* of equivalence that typifies interlingual relationships.

A fundamental difference emerges from the historical development of the two lexical items and their respective positions within the two language systems. For the last 150 years Engl. *equivalence* has been used as a technical term in various exact sciences to denote a number of scientific phenomena or processes; in mathematics and formal logic it indicates a relationship of absolute symmetry and equality involving guaranteed reversibility.[8] At the same time however *equivalence* is also used as a Hard Word in the general vocabulary of English, where it has a much longer tradition: according to the *Oxford English Dictionary* the adjective *equivalent* goes back to 1460, while the noun *equivalence* was first recorded in 1541. In other words, the lexemes *equivalent/equivalence* are used in the English language both as sharply defined scientific terms and in the notoriously fuzzy area of general vocabulary to mean "of similar significance," "virtually the same thing" (*OED*). As the writings of J.R. Firth on translation indicate (Firth 1957), it was in the latter fuzzy sense and as an item of the general language that the word *equivalence* was originally used in English translation theory.[9]

German *Äquivalenz*, on the other hand, is a relatively new word, first recorded in Sanders' dictionary of 1876 with the definition "Wertgleichheit" (of equal value). In Weber's dictionary of 1908 the lexeme *Äquivalent* is found with the further definition "Entschädigung, Ersatz bietend" (compensation, offering a replacement). And finally *Äquivalenz* is also used as a technical term in various exact sciences (as is amply illustrated by the detailed entries in the 6-volume *Duden* and *Brockhaus-Wahrig*), including the disciplines of mathematics and formal logic, where it is semantically identical with the English term *equivalence*.

It is generally assumed (Wilss 1977) that the concept of *Äquivalenz* was taken over into German *Übersetzungswissenschaft* as a technical term from either mathematics or formal logic (or both) during the euphoria that hailed machine translation in the 1950s; this means that from the outset the element of reversability was salient, as is indeed essential to machine translation. It was soon realized however, since linguistic items rarely show a one-to-one correspondence outside the narrow field of standardized terminol-

ogy, that for human translation the concept of *Äquivalenz* would have to be
reconsidered. And immediately the *Fremdwort Äquivalenz* was equated
with the morphologically transparent and more familiar word *Gleichwertigkeit* (equal value) from the everyday language (Reiss 1971:12).

What has not been realized here is that *Äquivalenz* and *Gleichwertigkeit* are
by no means interchangeable or semantically identical, and *Gleichwertigkeit*
bears even less resemblance to English *equivalence* than does the technical
term *Äquivalenz*: whereas *equivalence* indicates a quantitative approximation, *Gleichwertigkeit* denotes a qualitative evaluation (a component now
obsolete in Engl. *equivalence*). This is epitomized in sentences like:

> Mann und Frau sind gleichwertig (of equal worth),

as against the anomalous formations:

> *Mann und Frau sind äquivalent
> *Men and women are equivalent

The German and English terms expressing the central concept of translatology therefore show subtle but important differences, but the problem
does not end there. On closer investigation the attentive and critical reader
of the literature on translation theory can detect differences in the usage of
both *equivalence* and *Äquivalenz* even within the same language. In English
linguistics the issue was complicated by Chomsky's logically oriented term
equivalence as used in transformational grammar, which directly influenced
work written in English on contrastive linguistics,[10] and indirectly it also
affected translation theory; this may explain why in the writings of the
1960s *equivalence* was presented in more dogmatic terms than it had been
earlier by Firth or is now in more recent, pragmatically oriented writings.

With the realization that translation equivalence cannot be viewed in
terms of absolute symmetry, attempts were made to rethink the concept, to
qualify and classify it, leading to what can only be described as an explosive
proliferation of equivalence types. To show how differently this one term
can be interpreted, I shall here present a brief survey of the main
approaches to translation equivalence both in the English and the German
literature.

The discussion of the term *equivalence* was unleashed by an enigmatic
statement in Roman Jakobson's essay "On Linguistic Aspects of Translation" (1959): "Equivalence in difference is the cardinal problem of language

and the pivotal concern of linguistics. Like any receiver of verbal messages, the linguist acts as their interpreter." (1959:233f.) The phrase "equivalence in difference" was — ironically — taken over as a focal concept in German *Übersetzungswissenschaft* (Wilss 1977:157). Here it is glibly quoted or all too literally transcoded as "Äquivalenz in der Differenz," whereby however the linguists have *not* acted as the interpreters of the verbal messages concerned. It is this crucial element of understanding, of hermeneutics, that the linguistic theories of translation have underrated, ignored or even opposed: while German translation theory tends to view Jakobson's "equivalence in difference" as a scientifically rigorous equivalence type, it is in fact a profoundly paradoxical phrase expressing that dialectic tension which is a central problem of translation and will be crucial to our integrated approach (see 3.4 below).

Another influential concept was Nida's dichotomy "formal vs. dynamic equivalence" (1964). His celebrated example from Bible translation is the phrase "Lamb of God," whereby "Lamb" symbolizes innocence, especially in the context of sacrifice. A literal translation ("formal equivalence") would create problems in a culture, such as that of the Eskimos, where the lamb is an unfamiliar animal and symbolizes nothing. The "dynamic equivalent" in this case would be "Seal of God," the seal being naturally associated with innocence in the Eskimo culture. It was this pragmatic, approximative approach that Nida had in mind when he formulated the phrase "closest natural equivalent" in his definition of translation quoted above.

Catford's concept of equivalence is more general and abstract. He makes a distinction between "formal correspondence" and "textual equivalence" (1965:27), which he defines as follows:

> A textual equivalent is any TL text or portion of text which is observed on a particular occasion, by methods described below, to be the equivalent of a given SL text or portion of text.

— a circular definition which leads nowhere. One of the methods described by Catford runs as follows:

> The discovery of textual equivalents is based on the authority of a competent bilingual informant or translator.

As anyone with experience in translation knows all too well, the opinions of the most competent translators can diverge considerably, and the above suggestion is — for a rigorously scientific discipline — hopelessly inadequate. Furthermore, Catford bases his approach on isolated and even absurdly simplistic sentences of the type propagated in theories of transformational grammar as well as on isolated words; from such examples he derives "translation rules" which fall far short of the complex problems presented by real-life translation.

The first main centre of German *Übersetzungswissenschaft* was the Leipzig School,[11] where the concept of *Äquivalenz* flourished. The main contributions came from Kade (1968) and Filipec (1971). Kade presented a system of four clearly delimited equivalence types: *totale Äquivalenz* is found with completely identical terms as in standardized terminology; *fakultative Äquivalenz* (one-to-many correspondence) is exemplified in German *Spannung* as against English *voltage, tension, suspense, stress, pressure; approximative Äquivalenz* (one-to-part-of-one correspondence) is present in German *Himmel* as against *heaven/sky*, while *Null-Äquivalenz* is attested in the case of culture-bound items (such as *wicket* or *Privatdozent*). Kade's work mainly involved special language translation, where such a quantitative approach might sometimes apply; his system of equivalence types was however intended to include general language translation, for whose complexities it is again inadequate. Another feature of Kade's approach is the implicit assumption that the language system can be equated with the concrete realization in a text (a problem which will be discussed under 2.3 below), and it was he who presented the concept of "potential equivalents" from which the translator selects the "optimal equivalent" for the case in question — another oversimplification of the translation process which linguistically oriented translation theorists uncritically included in their own discussions (cf. Reiss 1971; Diller and Kornelius 1978). All in all, Kade's system of equivalence types ultimately hampered further development because it was limited to the level of individual words — an approach which clearly reflected the atomistic linguistic orientation still dominant at the time. Against that the concept presented by Filipec (1971), who gave "structural equivalence," or equivalence of the entire text, priority over individual lexical equivalents, represents a remarkable step forward.

In West Germany the "Äquivalenzdiskussion" reached its climax during the 1970s (cf. Wilss 1977:156), although this mainly consisted in adopting and classifying the already existing concepts and terms discussed above, and little was added that was new or original. Koller's five equivalence types, for example (*denotativ*, *konnotativ*, *textnormativ*, *pragmatisch*, *formal*), as presented in 1979, represent little more than a reshuffling of other equivalence types, and the terms themselves are far from watertight.[12]

Around 1980 however, a number of studies appeared which viewed the concept of equivalence in a new light and at the same time exemplified the essential — but nonetheless up to now still undetected — difference between the English term *equivalence* and German *Äquivalenz*. This becomes especially clear if one compares two studies which correlate the concept of *equivalence* and its would-be counterpart *Äquivalenz* with the problems of literary translation: Norbert Hofmann's *Redundanz und Äquivalenz in der literarischen Übersetzung, dargestellt an fünf deutschen Übersetzungen des* Hamlet (1980) and Robert de Beaugrande's *Factors in a Theory of Poetic Translating* (1978), illustrated by the author's own translations of Rilke's *Duineser Elegien*. Hofmann's approach is based on Nida, Kade and Reiss, whereby the concept of equivalence is used as a narrow, purpose-specific and rigorously scientific criterion. Against that Beaugrande's concept of equivalence — "by which I mean that the translation is a valid representative of the original in the communicative act" (1978: 14) — is so broad that it plays only a minor role in his "rule-guided strategies of translation." In 1981 Stephen Ross, in an essay on the complexity of translation, went even further by suggesting that the term *equivalence* should be replaced by the even vaguer term *similarity*. In the same year, in his book *Approaches to Translation*, Peter Newmark declared with refreshing candour: "Other subjects, such as the unit of translation, translation equivalence, translation invariance (...) I regard as dead ducks — either too theoretical or too arbitrary" (1981:x). The essential difference between the English and the German concept of equivalence emerges clearly from these remarks and can be summarized as follows: while *Äquivalenz* — as a narrow, purpose-specific and rigorously scientific constant — has become increasingly static and one-dimensional, *equivalence* (leaving aside the TG-influenced concepts of the 1960s) has become increasingly approximative and vague to the point of complete insignificance.

That might seem a logical end to the entire discussion, but a corollary is necessary due to the subsequent resuscitation of the term *Äquivalenz* in Germany: Neubert's paper read at the Saarbrücken Conference in 1983 (Neubert 1984) indicates that the Leipzig School still clings to the concept, though his "text-bound equivalence" represents a radical readjustment of the orthodox Leipzig approach, and he has continued to use the term in his more recent work (Neubert 1986). Finally, in Reiss and Vermeer 1984, Reiss attempted to revitalize the term by a modified definition and by an analogy with the equivalence phenomenon in electrical engineering (Reiss and Vermeer 1984:82), although other German-speaking scholars reject the concept of equivalence outright as a concept unsuitable for translation studies (as for example Hönig and Kussmaul 1982; Holz-Mänttäri 1984; see also Paepcke and Forget 1981 and Schmitt 1986). In this study the view is also taken that equivalence is unsuitable as a basic concept in translation theory: the term *equivalence*, apart from being imprecise and ill-defined (even after a heated debate of over twenty years) presents an illusion of symmetry between languages which hardly exists beyond the level of vague approximations and which distorts the basic problems of translation.

1.2.4 *Translation as manipulation*

The second major school of thought in Europe views translation studies as a branch of Comparative Literature. This school is centred round the Dutch-speaking area and is represented mainly by scholars such as André Lefevere, José Lambert and Theo Hermans, but it also includes Susan Bassnett in England and some Israeli scholars such as Gideon Toury. For a long time much of their work was virtually inaccessible, as it existed in the form of mimeographed manuscripts, unpublished doctoral dissertations, conference proceedings or local publications with only a limited circulation.[13] This was probably the reason why their approach to translation seemed somewhat fragmented and incoherent to the outsider and was barely heeded by the linguistically oriented German theorists. Then however some leading members of the group published an anthology of essays with the title *The Manipulation of Literature. Studies in Literary Translation* (Hermans 1985), on the basis of which they were dubbed the "Manipulation School." This is indeed an apt characterization of their approach; in the introduction to the book Theo Hermans writes: "From the point of view of the target literature, all translation implies a degree of manipulation of the source text for a certain purpose." (1985:9) Hence their starting-point is the exact opposite of that represented by the linguistically oriented school as discussed above: not intended equivalence but admitted manipulation.

In their English publications, the scholars call their subject Translation Studies, but their Dutch name for it is *vertaalwetenschap*. Despite the formal similarity of the term to the German word *Übersetzungswissenschaft*, their approach has little in common with that of the German school. On the contrary, these scholars nearly all work in Comparative Literature and confine themselves exclusively to literary translation, which the linguistically oriented German theorists dismissed as being deviant language inaccessible to rigorous analysis or scientific explanation. Conversely the scholars from the Low Countries explicitly reject the influence of linguistics for their field of studies:

> Linguistics has undoubtedly benefited our understanding of translation as far as the treatment of *unmarked, non-literary texts* is concerned. But as it proved too restricted in scope to be of much use to literary studies generally — witness the frantic attempts in recent years to construct a text linguistics — and unable to deal with the manifold complexities of literary works, it became obvious that it could not serve as a proper basis for the study of literary translation either. (Hermans 1985:10, emphasis added)

Given this attitude one is justified in describing the two approaches to translation as "mutually exclusive": each side dismisses the other's field of study in strikingly vague and general terms as a domain outside its own aims, interests and responsibility. There remains the question as to what exactly is meant by "free play" with language on the one hand, and what an "unmarked text" is on the other.

The approach of the "Manipulation School" is based on the concept of the literary polysystem going back to the Russian Formalists and the Prague Structuralists, but in particular as developed by the Tel Aviv scholar Itamar Even-Zohar (1978 and 1979):

> Making use of insights from the field of general systemics, the study of how systems work, Even-Zohar and his colleagues have posited that 'literature' in a given society is a collection of various systems, a system-of-systems or polysystem, in which diverse genres, schools, tendencies, and what have you are constantly jockeying for position, competing with each other for readership, but also for prestige and power. Seen in this light, 'literature' is no longer the stately and fairly static thing it tends to be for the canonists, but a highly kinetic situation in which things are constantly changing. (Holmes 1985:150)

Such a polysystem is not only characterized by constant shifts and changes, but also by internal oppositions, including those between "primary" and "secondary" models and types. Such primary texts are the innovative ones, "introducing into a literary polysystem new ideas, new methods, new ways of looking at literature and the world, that were not present in it before" (Holmes 1985:151). The secondary texts are the conservative ones which confirm and uphold the existing system.

In this view, literary translation is seen as one of the elements participating in the constant struggle for survival and domination, and the Israeli scholars emphasize that translations have frequently played a primary, creative and innovative role within their literary systems. Hence in this approach, translation is seen essentially as a text-type in its own right, as an integral part of the target culture and not merely as a reproduction of another text.

From this essentially target-oriented starting-point, the "Manipulation" scholars have developed their own tenets, methods and theoretical models. Their emphasis on the target text naturally leads to a primarily *descriptive* approach which explicitly rejects the normative and evaluative attitudes of both traditional translation theory and linguistically oriented translatology. A further logical development is the shift of emphasis from the translation *process* and the problems underlying it to the *result*, the translated text as a historical fact. Thus beyond the basic theoretical framework, the studies of this group are concrete and empirical, with a strong emphasis on practical fieldwork and case studies. This means that the writings of the "Manipulation School" concentrate on describing and analyzing translations (Lefevere 1984), comparing different translations of the same work (though again descriptively rather than on an evaluative basis), on investigating the reception of translations (Vanderauwera 1985), and on tracing broad historical surveys (Van Gorp 1985; Lambert et al. 1985; Toury 1986); in short, they have much in common with conventional studies in Comparative Literature except that they deal with translations rather than original works.

Within the theoretical framework of literary translation however, some of the ideas presented by the scholars from the Low Countries are challenging indeed. The violent rejection of what is described as "the normative and source-oriented approaches typical of most traditional thinking about translation" (Hermans 1985:9) even involves the rejection of translation critique in general and basically too of translators' training institutes with their inevitably normative and evaluative approach.[14] Indeed, Toury has gone so far as to plead for an untrained "native translator" (Toury 1984) as a "non-conformist-to-be" (Toury 1980a). Taken to its extreme, this view implies that any text is to be accepted as a translation of another text if it is declared as such, and is hence to be treated by the scholar as an accepted part of the literary system. One is left wondering whether the element of evaluation and judgement can ever be completely dispensed with.

On the other hand, the broad panoramic view of the literary polysys-tem as against the fixation on the single item within the individual text, rep-resents a welcome and necessary readjustment from the myopic perspective of the equivalence proponents. Indeed, what Hermans calls the "new paradigm for the study of literary translation" (1985:10) seems to have great potential for translation theory as long as it is allowed to be fully exploited. What is envisaged is:

> ... a view of literature as a *complex and dynamic system*, a conviction that there should be a continual *interplay between theoretical models and practi-cal case studies*; an approach to literary translation which is descriptive, target-oriented, functional and systemic; and an interest in the *norms and constraints* that govern the *production and reception* of translations, in the *relation* between translation and *other types of text-processing*, and in the place and role of translation both *within a given literature* and in the *interaction between literatures*. (1985:10f., emphasis added)

The above survey of literary and linguistic orientations in the history of translation theory leads us to some interesting conclusions. Firstly, it is striking how repetitive some of the thinking, the concepts and the terms have been: the historical dichotomy, whether the words used are "faithful vs. free," "word vs. sense" or "source-oriented vs. target-oriented," has basically the same identity, even in the new paradigm developed in the Low Countries, and the same principles and guidelines for a good translation have been formulated with almost identical words at least since the Renais-sance. Secondly, all the theorists, whether linguists or literary scholars, for-mulate theories for their own area of translation; little attempt is made to bridge the gap between literary and "other" translation. Thirdly, neither the perspective of literary studies nor the methods of linguistics have pro-vided any substantial help in furthering translation studies as a whole. What is needed is a basic reorientation in thinking, a revision of the traditional forms of categorization, and an integrated approach that considers transla-tion in its entirety, and not only certain forms of it.

1.3 Categorization and text-type

The tendency to categorize is innate in man and essential to all scientific development, and to be able to categorize we need concepts. Our discussion so far has centred round concepts (such as the unstable concept of equivalence) and the categories that ensue from them. Looking back at the definitions and descriptions quoted so far in this study, we see that these too fall into distinct categories, the most striking being the *dichotomy*, or rigid polarization. In 20th century linguistics the dichotomy as a mode of categorization is associated especially with Saussure, whose distinction between form and substance in linguistic items is directly reflected in Nida's dichotomy of formal vs. dynamic equivalence and Catford's dichotomy of formal correspondence vs. textual equivalence. Another kind of categorization is the *typology*, or system of box-like compartments, as in Kade's system of equivalence types, each of these being clear-cut and sharply delimited from the others.

Both the dichotomy and the typology are fundamental to the classical theory of categorization that is part of our Western culture. In recent years however, the validity of this theory has been challenged within a number of cognitive sciences: relevant for our present purpose is the work done in psychology by Eleanor Rosch and its development within linguistics by George Lakoff.[15]

1.3.1 *Prototype and gestalt*

In his study *Categories and Cognitive Models* (1982), Lakoff presents a brief survey of the classical theory of categorization: this entails *clear boundaries* between categories without borderline cases or fuzziness of any kind, *shared properties* as conditions for category membership (the so-called "checklist theory"), *uniformity* among all members of the category, *inflexibility* of category boundaries, *internal definition*, strictly *objective conditions* for category membership, and the reductionist principle of ultimate *primitives* (Lakoff 1982:15).

Nowhere is this objectivist and reductionist approach better illustrated than in the method of formalized componential analysis which up to very recently dominated lexical semantics. A well-known example is the word *bachelor*, which — as presented in the semantic theory of transformational grammar (cf. Katz 1972) — is reducible to the components (or primitives) + MALE, + ADULT, – MARRIED.

On the basis of experiments, Eleanor Rosch set out to test the classical theory of categorization as expounded in objectivist psychology, where *experiential aspects* (perception, mental imagery, bodily experiences, desires and expectations, social experiences, understanding one thing in terms of another) were ruled out completely. Rosch's experiments disproved the classical theory on all counts and led to her own theory of natural categorization (1973), according to which human beings categorize in the form of *prototypes* — in other words, the natural category has a focus or "hard core" and fades off at the edges. In Rosch's category BIRD, for example, robins are judged to be more representative than penguins and ostriches, and desk chairs are judged to be more representative of the category CHAIR than are rocking chairs, beanbag chairs or electric chairs (Lakoff 1982:16).

Rosch's findings also influenced American semantic theory, where the recently developed "prototype semantics" challenges the validity of the "checklist theory" as propagated by the generative school. This means that the lexical item *bachelor* cannot be reduced to the sum of three simple components, but also depends on a prototype conditioned by sociocultural factors. Fillmore maintains:

> The noun *bachelor* can be defined as an unmarried adult man, but the noun clearly exists as a motivated device for categorizing people only in the context of a human society in which certain expectations about marriage and marriageable age obtain. Male participants in long-term unmarried couplings would not ordinarily be described as bachelors; a boy abandoned in the jungle and grown to maturity away from contact with human society would not be called a bachelor; John Paul II is not properly thought of as a bachelor. (1982:34)

In other words, the Pope may be an unmarried male adult, but he does no represent the bachelor-prototype; he is rather a "borderline case" on the "blurred edge" of the category BACHELOR.

The notion of the "blurred edge" as applied to concepts is of course b no means new: this phrase was used by Wittgenstein in his *Philosophica Investigations* of 1953. Another of Wittgenstein's celebrated notions, that o "family resemblances," is also confirmed by Rosch's experiments, where i is used in the sense of "perceived similarities between representative an nonrepresentative members" of the category concerned (Lakoff 1982:16)

Thus category membership is not dependent on necessary and fixed conditions, as in the classical theory, but rather on "clusters of attributes that characterize the most representative members" (Lakoff 1982:16).

A second important conclusion Rosch made in her experiments is derived from what she calls *basic level results*, her basic categories being situated between superordinate and subordinate. Thus *chair* represents the basic level between the superordinate *furniture* and the subordinate *rocking-chair*. The use of such taxonomies is of course nothing new in linguistic theory (and was essential to structural semantics — cf. Snell-Hornby 1983), but of interest for the present study are Rosch's conclusions and the research they led to. Rosch contends that the basic categories (such as *chair*) do not depend on the objects themselves, but on the way people interact with them, perceive and use them. Hence while a chair is imagined as something to sit on, there is no such interactional image connected with the more abstract superordinate category *furniture*. Rosch's notion of the basic level category stimulated research in ethnobiology by Brent Berlin (Berlin et al. 1974), who concludes that this "folk-generic level" (in his terminology) is in several respects psychologically basic: at that level languages have simple names, categories have greater cultural significance and things are more easily remembered, but above all — and for our purposes this is the essential point:

> At that level, things are perceived *holistically, as a single gestalt*, while for identification at a lower level, specific details have to be picked out. (Lakoff 1982:20, emphasis added)

It is the holistic principle of the *gestalt* that will be essential in our integrated approach to translation, which for far too long was thought to be merely a matter of isolatable words. Like the notion of "blurred edges," the gestalt-concept links up with the European tradition: the main principle of the school of Gestalt psychology, itself based on experimental studies carried out by Max Wertheimer, Wolfgang Köhler and Kurt Kofka (Wertheimer 1912), is that the whole is more than the mere sum of its parts, and an analysis of the parts cannot provide an understanding of the whole. This principle — a foregone conclusion in literary studies — was until very recently totally ignored by philologists and linguists: the study of language, and with it the "scientific," linguistically oriented translation theory, remained atomistic, fragmented and out of touch with language in its concrete realization. The change took place in the 1970s, mainly — as in the case of the prototype and gestalt — via other disciplines such as sociology (sociolinguistics), moral philosophy (the speech act theory of Austin and Searle), ethnology and psychology, and with the development of text-linguistics a more holistic approach to language was made possible.[16] In America, Berlin's ethnobiological notion of the gestalt was taken up and developed as a linguistic concept by Lakoff in his study "Linguistic Gestalts" (1977). At the same time the Finnish linguist Raimo Anttila published an essay drawing on the same principles of Gestalt psychology with the title "Dynamic fields and linguistic structure: A proposal for a Gestalt linguistics" (1977), and in Germany a book was published by Stephan Langhoff with the title *Gestaltlinguistik* (1980). Even if the term *Gestalt linguistics* is used in only a few individual studies, the holistic principle itself has become increasingly dominant in the study of language over the last few years, and in recent translation theory it is of primary importance.

1.3.2 *Text-typologies and the prototypology*

The conclusion drawn by Lakoff in *Categories and Cognitive Models* is that the theory of natural categorization "requires not only a very different theory of categories, but a different world-view to go with it" (1982:22). Central to this new theory are *experiential* aspects: mental imagery, memory, social functions, human intentions, gestalt perception — "all matters that have to do with human interaction with and functioning in the world, rather than with objective properties of the world" (Lakoff 1982:22).

Language as part of the world: this notion is central to the integrated approach adopted in the present study, and at the same time it represents the point of departure from the "world-view" that dominated the linguistically oriented translation theory.

As we have already seen, the main categorization-types governing translation theory have been the dichotomy and the typology, the latter being a system of box-like compartments as in Kade's equivalence-types. The use of the typology in translation theory extends beyond the concept of equivalence however: it was of basic importance as a tool for categorizing texts.

In her pioneering study *Möglichkeiten und Grenzen der Übersetzungskritik* (1971) Katharina Reiss aims at deriving strictly objective criteria for assessing the quality of translations. Her approach is based on a translation-related text-typology (1971:31ff.), whereby the text-type is presented as a "literary category of translation critique" (1971:52f.). Reiss' typology is founded on Karl Bühler's organon-model (Bühler 1965:28; 1990:35), where the three functions of language are shown to be *Darstellung* (representation), *Ausdruck* (expression) and *Appell* (appeal). From this three-fold division Reiss derives corresponding "dimensions of language" and corresponding text-types.[17] This she represents in the following diagram:

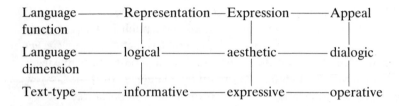

Language———————Representation—Expression————————Appeal
function | | |

Language————— logical—————— aesthetic————— dialogic
dimension | | |

Text-type————— informative——— expressive————operative

Reiss then offers criteria for translation according to the respective text-type: a metaphor in an "expressive" text, for example, must be rendered as a metaphor in the translation, but this is not necessary for a metaphor in an "informative" text (1971:62). The same principle applies for idioms: the Spanish idiom "miente más que el gobierno," for example, would — according to Reiss — be rendered into German as "er lügt allzuviel (he often lies)" in an "informative" text, whereas in an "expressive" text a better translation would be the German idiom "er lügt wie gedruckt (he lies like mad)" (1971:81f.). Such prescriptive generalizations can be extremely misleading, and indeed Reiss has been severely criticized (cf. Koller 1979) for being too rigid. As Reiss herself actually indicates (1971:32), most texts are in fact hybrid forms, multi-dimensional structures with a blend of sometimes seemingly conflicting features: Shakespeare's sonnets contain technical terminology of his day, while modern economic texts abound in lexicalized metaphor, and advertisements (which would be categorized by Reiss as strictly "operative" (cf. Reiss 1976)) are characterized by the varying methods they use to present information. As a starting-point Bühler's model undoubtedly has great possibilities for translation theory; as a frame of reference for objective criteria Reiss' typology, as presented here, though modified in Reiss (1976), is too clear-cut for real-life translation in all its complexity. What is wrong is the use of box-like categories as a kind of prescriptive grid, creating an illusion of the scientific objectivity that was required of academic thinking at the time.

Reiss's text-typology demonstrates the shortcomings of the classical theory of categorization. In its concrete realization language cannot be reduced to a system of static and clear-cut categories. In the present study the rigid typology of the objectivist and reductionist tradition will therefore be replaced by the *prototypology*,[18] a dynamic, gestalt-like system of relationships, whereby the various headings represent an idealized, prototypical focus and the grid-system gives way to blurred edges and overlappings. Blend-forms are part of the conceptual system and not the exception. Whereas the typology aims at separation and sharp delimitation, the prototypology aims at focussing and at subtle differentiation.

1.4 An integrated approach

The ideas discussed so far will now be presented in concrete form as a basis for an integrated concept of translation studies. In the diagram on the following page a system of relationships is established between basic text-types — as prototypes — and the crucial aspects of translation. On the horizontal plane the diagram represents a spectrum or cline,[19] where sharp divisions have been replaced by the notion of gradual transition, hence no demarcation lines have been drawn in. At the same time, on the vertical plane, the diagram represents a *stratificational model* which, in accordance with the gestalt-principle, proceeds from the most general level (A) at the top, downwards to the most particular level (F) at the bottom — or, in other words, from the macro- to the micro-level.

Level A presents the conventional areas of translation which up to now have been kept all too separate: on the left literary translation, traditionally the province of poets and scholars and once the only area thought worthy of the theorist, and on the right special language translation, traditionally inferior and the main concern of the translation schools. "General language translation" is still a vague concept which up to now has only been negatively defined as "not literary" and "not technical,"[20] but which is nonetheless implicitly the concern of the linguistically oriented *Übersetzungswissenschaft*. In this concept the historical dichotomy has been replaced by a fluid spectrum, whereby, for example, prototypically literary devices such as word-play and alliteration can be accommodated both in "general" newspaper texts (cf. 2.4.1 below) and in the language of advertising, and conversely prototypically technical terms from the language of science or cul-

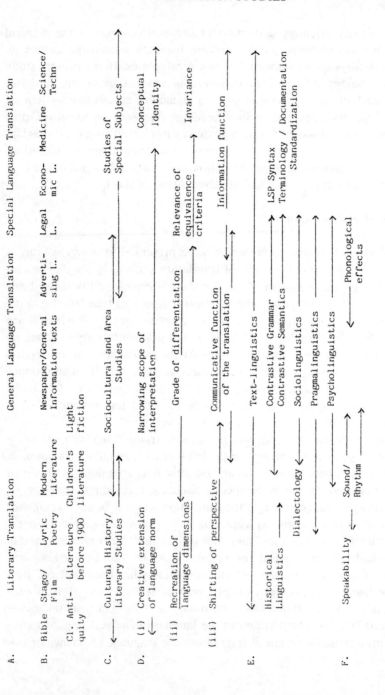

Text-type and relevant criteria for translation

ture-bound items from the "general" area of politics or everyday living can be explained and interpreted as literary devices (cf. 4.2 below).

Level B presents a prototypology of the basic text-types, from the Bible to the language of modern technology, which are the main concern of the translator. While traditional theory concentrated on the items situated at the extreme left of the spectrum, the Bible, the monuments of Classical Antiquity and the great works of the European tradition, particularly Shakespeare's plays, only a few of these areas have been given detailed attention in modern theory, and even then the focus has been limited to specific aspects (for Bible translation see Nida and Taber 1969, for lyric poetry Levy 1969 and Beaugrande 1978). The special problems of children's literature and stage-translation until recently only received scant attention (cf. Verch 1976, Reiss 1982 on children's literature and Snell-Hornby 1984, Bassnett-McGuire 1985 and Schultze 1986 on the translation of drama). At the other end of the scale are the special language text-types, the main fare of the modern professional translator; in the training institutes the major areas are law, economics, medicine, science and technology, and these are now being dealt with intensively in academic studies (cf. Schmitt 1986; Stellbrink 1984a and 1985; Gerzymisch-Arbogast 1986 and 1987). On the diagram limited space permitted only a narrow selection of basic text-types; there are of course many others, along with numerous blend forms (cf. 4.1 below).

Level C shows the non-linguistic disciplines — or areas of so-called "extralinguistic reality" — which are inseparably bound up with translation. The terms are placed at the point of the cline where they are thought to apply most, but again, we are concerned here with the dynamic concept of focus and not with grid-like compartments involving rigid classification; the arrows indicate the range of application or, where they overlap, interaction. Essential for special language translation, for example, is specialized factual knowledge of the subject concerned, while literary translation presupposes a background in literary studies and cultural history. A necessary precondition for all translation is knowledge of the sociocultural background (see 2.1 below), both of the source culture and the target culture concerned.

Level D names important aspects and criteria governing the translation process itself, an extremely complex area which at this point is dealt with only briefly, as most of them form the main topic of chapters to follow. D(i) focusses on the source text: crucial here is the *understanding* of the text (see 2.1 and 4.1 below), which does not simply involve familiarity with words and structures, but presupposes the ability to penetrate the *sense* of the text, both as a complex multidimensional whole and at the same time in its relationship to the cultural background (see 3.3 below). With certain special language texts involving standardized concepts (particularly in science and technology) the scope of interpretation is narrowed down considerably. D(ii) names focal criteria for the envisaged translation: the notion of invariance can only apply in cases of conceptual identity (standardized terminology), while the concept of equivalence is here still considered to be of some relevance for certain types of special language translation where the focus is on isolatable lexical items (see 3.5.1 below). Basically however, our conception of translation supports the more dynamic approach pioneered by Hönig and Kussmaul (1982), whose dominant criterion is the *communicative function* of the target text (the stage indicated in D(iii)), which governs what they call the "notwendigen Grad der Differenzierung" (the necessary degree of precision) (see Hönig and Kussmaul 1982:58ff. and 2.2 below). With texts involving the *creative extension* of the language norm (2.3 below) — this applies mainly but not exclusively to literary texts — translation involves *recreating* language *dimensions* and results in a shift of *perspective* in the target text (2.4 below).

Level E names those areas of linguistics which are relevant for translation. Of basic importance is text-linguistics in all its aspects, from the analysis of the macrostructure (see 3.2 below), thematic progression and sentence perspective (cf. Gerzymisch-Arbogast 1986) to coherence and cohesion. Older literature requires knowledge of Historical Linguistics, while special language translation presupposes familiarity with work in terminology and access to data-banks. Contrastive Linguistics, both in syntax and lexicology, has great potential for translation theory, although up to now its results in this respect have been meagre (cf. 3.5 below). Other disciplines of relevance for translation as an act of communication within a specific situational context would be sociolinguistics (as the study of language varieties), pragmalinguistics (in particular the speech act theory, cf. 3.4 below), and psycholinguistics (as regards the interdependence of language, experience and thought, cf. 2.1 below). And finally, the lowest level F names phonological aspects of specific relevance for certain areas of translation, as for example, speakability in stage translation, alliteration and rhythm in advertising language.

With this prototypological framework the foundations have been laid for our conception of translation studies as an integrated and independent discipline that covers all kind of translation, from literary to technical. In this view, translation draws on many disciplines, but is not equal to the sum total of their overlapping areas and is not dependent on any one of them. As a discipline in its own right, translation studies needs to develop its own methods based, not on outside models and conventions from other disciplines, but on the complexities of translation. The present study is intended as a step in that direction.

At this stage I should like to summarize, in four briefly worded hypotheses, the results of what has been established so far:

(1) Translation studies should not be considered a mere offshoot of another discipline or sub-discipline (whether Applied Linguistics or Comparative Literature): both the translator and the translation theorist are rather concerned with a world *between* disciplines, languages and cultures.

(2) Whereas linguistics has gradually widened its field of interest from the micro- to the macro-level, translation studies, which is concerned essentially with texts against their situational and cultural background, should adopt the reverse perspective: as maintained by the gestalt psychologists, an analysis of parts cannot provide an understanding of the whole, which must be analyzed from "the top down "

(3) Translation studies has been hampered by classical modes of categorization, which operate with rigid dividing-lines, binary opposites, antitheses and dichotomies. Frequently these are mere academic constructs which paralyze the finer differentiation required in all aspects of translation studies. In our approach the typology is replaced by the prototypology, admitting blends and blurred edges, and the dichotomy gives way to the concept of a spectrum or cline against which phenomena are situated and focussed.

(4) While the classic approach to the study of language and translation has been to isolate phenomena (mainly words) and study them in depth, translation studies is essentially concerned with a web of relationships, the importance of individual items being decided by their relevance in the larger context of text, situation and culture.

Notes

1. Examples of this type are the Department of Slavic Languages and Literatures at the University of Pennsylvania and the Department of European Languages and Literature at the University of Hawaii.

2. The newer Departments of Linguistics in North America are further results of this trend; the "Institute für Allgemeine Sprachwissenschaft" in German-speaking universities in Europe tend to preserve the traditional approach of Comparative Philology.

3. This date refers, not to the older bilingual word lists (cf. Snell-Hornby 1986b), but to the fully developed "translation agencies" as described in Mounin 1967; 23.

4. A typical example of this being the Strasbourg oaths in Old High German.

5. See Klein-Braley 1982 and Kornelius 1982.

6. The German version of the famous essay by Ortega y Gasset is reprinted in Störig 1973:296-321.

7. Cf. Beaugrande 1978 and 1988.

8. In the *Encyclopaedia Britannica* it is defined as follows: *"equivalence*, also called *equivalence of propositions*, in logic and mathematics, refers to the formation of a proposition from two others which are linked by the phrase 'if, and only if.' The equivalence formed from two propositions p and q also may be defined by the statement 'p is a necessary and sufficient condition for q.'" This kind of reversability is essential for machine translation, but it is now agreed that it hardly applies to human translation.

9. Cf. Firth (1970:5): "Livingstone notes in his *Last Journals* that among a certain African tribe clapping the hands in various ways is the polite way of saying 'Allow me,' 'I beg pardon,' 'Permit me to pass,' 'Thanks;' it is resorted to in respectful introduction and leave-taking, and also is *equivalent* to 'Hear, hear.'" Note also Firth 1968: 112: "It should be remembered that *so-called translation equivalents* between two languages are never *really equivalent."* (Emphasis added.)

10. See especially Krzeszowski 1971, where the term *equivalence* is used to cover both translation and abstract elements of linguistics. For the use of the term in contrastive grammar see Hellinger 1977.

11. As was represented in the "Sektion Angewandte Sprachwissenschaft" of the Karl-Marx-Universität. Many pioneering ideas were published in supplements to the journal *Fremdsprachen* and were taken up in the Western stream of translation theory (see Newmark 1981).

12. This emerges clearly from Vermeer's discussion of Koller's *formale Äquivalenz* in Vermeer 1983:89ff.

13. These include Holmes et al. 1978 (now out of print) and Toury 1980.

14. Cf. Holmes 1985: 152: "For those who now think of themselves as *translation scholars*, are *not primarily concerned with the day-to-day problems of training young translators*, and have come from a *background in literary studies*, the attraction of the polysystem approach is strong." (Emphasis added.) Such a sharp distinction between "translation scholars" on the one hand, and "translator trainers" on the other hardly promotes a unified discipline of translation studies.

15.   See especially Lakoff 1977 and 1982; also Lakoff and Johnson 1980.

16.   In practice, only those branches of text-linguistics are relevant for translation which concentrate on concrete texts as against abstract models (cf. Beaugrande and Dressler 1981 and Stolze 1982:55ff.). In this study the term *text-linguistics* is used in the concrete sense in its relevance for translation.

17.   In this study (see 2.4 below) the term *dimension* is extended beyond the threefold division proposed by Reiss. The English term *text-type* as used here includes German *Texttyp* (as used by Reiss) and *Textsorte* (as in diagram on p. 32).

18.   The term *Prototypologie* goes back to Neubert (Brussels 1984, personal communication), who applies the concept of the prototype to lexicography in Neubert 1986a.

19.   This conception of the *cline* as well as that of the *stratificational model* go back to the British linguist M.A.K. Halliday (see Halliday 1976).

20.   The German term *Gemeinsprache* is matched in English by both *general language* (as against technical language) and *ordinary language* (as against literary language), cf. 4.1 and 4.2 below.

2. Translation as a cross-cultural event

2.1 Language and culture

It has for centuries been taken for granted that translation merely takes place between languages. This assumption unleashed the word vs. sense debate in traditional theory and lies at the heart of the concept of equivalence. It is also apparent in dictionary definitions of translation, as in the meagre sentence accorded to the headword *translation* in the *Encyclopaedia Britannica*: "*translation*, the act or process of rendering what is expressed in one language or set of symbols by means of another language or set of symbols" (*Micropaedia* 10:93). In the *Macropaedia* translation is not even thought worthy of autonomous treatment, but is dealt with very briefly under a sub-heading of a sub-section of the article on language — an attitude which is the rule rather than the exception and which the translator and the translation theorist have had to learn to live with. One aspect of the *Encyclopaedia Britannica's* modest contribution on translation does however give cause for optimism: unlike the traditional approach in linguistics (which for a long time endeavoured to draw a sharp dividing-line between language and what was called "extralinguistic reality"), language is not seen as an isolated phenomenon suspended in a vacuum but as an integral part of culture; the sub-section of which the few paragraphs on translation form a sub-division happens in fact to have the same title as this present chapter: Language and culture.

Culture is here not understood in the narrower sense of man's advanced intellectual development as reflected in the arts, but in the broader anthropological sense to refer to all *socially conditioned* aspects of human life (cf. Hymes 1964). This concept of culture was defined by the American ethnologist Ward H. Goodenough as follows:

> As I see it, a society's culture consists of whatever it is one has to know or
> believe in order to operate in a manner acceptable to its members, and do
> so in any role that they accept for any one of themselves. Culture, being

what people have to learn as distinct from their biological heritage, must consist of the end product of learning: knowledge, in a most general, if relative, sense of the term. By this definition, we should note that culture is not a material phenomenon; it does not consist of things, people, behavior, or emotions. It is rather an organization of these things. It is the forms of things that people have in mind, their models for perceiving, relating, and otherwise interpreting them. As such, the things people say and do, their social arrangements and events, are products or by-products of their culture as they apply it to the task of perceiving and dealing with their circumstances. To one who knows their culture, these things and events are also signs signifying the cultural forms or models of which they are material representations (...). (1964:36)

In Germany, within the recently developed, culturally contrastive discipline called Cross-cultural Communication, Heinz Göhring has adapted Goodenough's definition as follows:

Culture is everything one needs to know, master and feel in order to judge where people's behaviour conforms to or deviates from what is expected from them in their social roles, and in order to make one's own behaviour conform to the expectations of the society concerned — unless one is prepared to take the consequences of deviant behaviour.
(1977:10, my translation)

This new definition correlates with the concept of culture now prevalent in translation theory, particularly in the writings of Vermeer (see 2.2 below), and is the one adopted in this study.[1]

There are three important points common to both definitions quoted above, but which are especially prominent in Göhring's German adaptation: firstly, the concept of culture as a totality of knowledge, proficiency and perception;[2] secondly, its immediate connection with behaviour (or action) and events, and thirdly, its dependence on expectations and norms, whether those of social behaviour or those accepted in language usage. The first point is taken up in this present section, while the aspect of language as behaviour or action is included under 2.2 and the problem of norms is the subject of 2.3.

It was Wilhelm von Humboldt (1767-1835) who made the vital connection between language and culture, language and behaviour. For Humboldt language was something dynamic, an activity (energeia) rather than a static inventory of items as the product of activity (ergon). At the same time language is an expression both of the culture and the individuality of the speaker, who perceives the world through language. A century later, these ideas were echoed in American ethnolinguistics by Edward Sapir and Benjamin Lee Whorf, resulting in the Sapir-Whorf hypothesis, or principle of linguistic relativity, which maintains that thought does not "precede" language, but on the contrary it is conditioned by it. As with Humboldt, such conclusions were based on detailed study of barely accessible "exotic" languages such as those of the American Indians. Whorf maintained, for example, that the verb system in Hopi directly affected the speaker's conception of time (Whorf 1973:57-64). Similar conclusions have been reached in disciplines devoted to the study of ancient cultures: Sumerologists doing research into the civilization of Old Babylonia, for example, have put forward the principle of "Eigenbegrifflichkeit" (see Landsberger 1974), maintaining that the scholar can only approach some understanding of that world if he deals with it in its own concepts and in its own terms, without imposing 20th century European concepts and values upon it.

The principle of linguistic relativity has far-reaching implications for translation. Taken to its extreme, the notion that language conditions thought and that both are inextricably bound up with the individual culture of the community that speaks the language concerned would mean that ultimately translation is impossible.

The opposite point of view, ironically, also goes back to Wilhelm von Humboldt: it is the principle of language universals propagated by Chomsky and the school of generative grammar. Chomsky's concept of deep structure and surface structure is a development of Humboldt's theory of "inner" and "outer" form in language. In this view translation is a "recoding" or change of surface structure in representation of the — non-linguistic and ultimately universal — deep structure underlying it. Taken to its extreme, this principle means that everything is translatable.

Once again we are faced with a dichotomy of two extremes, and here too the answer lies, not in choosing which of the two conflicting alternatives to support, but in determining the point on the scale between them which is valid for the case in question. In other words, the extent to which a text is translatable varies with the *degree* to which it is embedded in its own specific culture, also with the distance that separates the cultural background of source text and target audience in terms of time and place. This "scale of translatability" closely reflects the continuum of texttypes and relevant criteria for translation shown on p. 32. Literary texts, especially those embedded in a culture of the distant past, tend to be less easily translatable than those texts dealing with the "universals" of modern science. Even this observation must however be modified, and again with reference to cultural background: while a report on atomic reactors is fully translatable among languages of societies that participate in modern technology, it is far less so if the envisaged target language is Tamil or Swahili. Similarly, to take an example from "general language" translation, an internal squabble among the Greens in Hesse is not easy to make intelligible to a typical reader of the conservative British *Daily Mail*. As these two examples show, the problems do not depend on the source text itself, but on the significance of the translated text for its readers as members of a certain culture, or of a sub-group within that culture, with the constellation of knowledge, judgement and perception they have developed from it.

The concept of culture as a totality of knowledge, proficiency and perception is fundamental in our approach to translation. If language is an integral part of culture, the translator needs not only proficiency in two languages, he must also be at home in two cultures. In other words, he must be bilingual and bicultural (cf. Vermeer 1986). The extent of his knowledge, proficiency and perception determines not only his ability to produce the target text, but also his understanding of the source text.

Hermeneutic theory, particularly in Germany, has long been bound up with translation theory (cf. the discussion of Heidegger and Buber in Kelly 1979:29ff.). Equally important for literary translation in particular is a more recent development, also with roots in Germany, known as *Rezeptionsästhetik* (theory of aesthetic response), investigating the role of the reader (Iser 1976, see 4.1 below). For our purposes it must be emphasized that the role of the translator as reader is an essentially active and creative one (cf. Hönig and Kussmaul 1982; Holz-Mänttäri 1984), and that understanding must not be equated with a passive "reception" of the text. In his fourfold "hermeneutic motion," George Steiner (1975:296) describes the "initiative trust, an investment of belief, underwritten by previous experience but epistemologically exposed and psychologically hazardous" which makes the translator "venture a leap." By including the fundamental element of experience, Steiner links his conception of the translator's understanding process with the work of two philosophers who have influenced recent work on translation in Germany: Edmund Husserl (1913) and Hans-Georg Gadamer with his concept of "Horizontverschmelzung" (fusion of horizons) (1960). Gadamer had a major influence on Paepcke's approach to translation (see especially Paepcke 1978, 1980, 1981) and on Stolze's work (1982, 1984 and 1986). The hermeneutic approach to translation with its experiential, interactive process of understanding as represented by Paepcke and Stolze also adheres to the holistic principles of the gestalt (see Stolze 1982:31f.) as described in this study. The unity of language, culture, experience and perception has likewise characterized some recent developments in linguistics: one such development — Fillmore's scenes-and-frames semantics, which draws on the prototype model as derived from world-knowledge and experience — is discussed below (3.3) as an approach directly relevant for translation.

2.2 Recent translation theories

Paepcke's approach to translation is fundamentally and essentially hermeneutic:

> Whatever has been written to the contrary, translation is based on understanding and not on theoretical constructs. (1985:1, my translation)

For the most recent translation theories understanding of the text is presupposed: the "unverstandene Übersetzung" envisaged in the 1960s by Gert Jäger as exponent of the Leipzig School has now been generally discarded, except for the limited and special case of machine translation (see 3.1 below). In most translation theory of the 1980s however, hermeneutic principles are not central, indeed, they are generally considered too vague to be a dependable basis for a theoretical approach.

What is dominant in the three new basic approaches recently presented in Germany (Hönig and Kussmaul 1982; Reiss and Vermeer 1984 and Holz-Mänttäri 1984) is the orientation towards cultural rather than linguistic transfer; secondly, they view translation, not as a process of transcoding, but as an *act* of *communication*; thirdly, they are all oriented towards the *function* of the *target text* (prospective translation) rather than prescriptions of the source text (retrospective translation); fourthly, they view the text as an *integral part of the world* and not as an isolated specimen of language. These basic similarities are so striking that it is not exaggerated to talk of a new orientation in translation theory.

The first of the three studies, Hönig and Kussmaul's *Strategie der Übersetzung* (1982) is actually intended as a text-book for students in the translation institutes, and the fact that it has a rich fund of illustrative examples and is written in a lively style enhances rather than detracts from its theoretical worth. The authors' approach is based on many years of teaching experience and work as professional translators, and represents a blend of theory and practice that was long overdue in translation studies. The translation strategies they develop do not concern us here, nor will the linguistic works be discussed on which the various methods are based: I am concentrating here only on their basic theoretical approach.[3] Hönig and Kussmaul's starting point is the conception of the text as what they call "der verbalisierte Teil eine Soziokultur" (the verbalized part of a socioculture) (1982:58): the text is embedded in a given situation, which is itself conditioned by its sociocultural background. The translation is then dependent on its function as a text "implanted" in the target culture, whereby there is the alternative of either preserving the original function of the source text in its own culture (*Funktionskonstanz*) or of changing the function to adapt to specified needs in the target culture (*Funktionsveränderung*). A striking example here is the case of advertising texts; the function of the text is preserved if the translation is likewise to be an advertisement addressed to potential customers with the intention of selling the product. It is changed if, for example, the text is used for information purposes, as on marketing conventions and strategies in the source culture. This observation implies something very important, which has up to now been ignored both in translator training and in traditional language departments: "the" translation per se does not exist, and neither does the "perfect translation." A translation is directly dependent on its prescribed function, which must be made clear by the client (in professional practice usually a foregone conclusion). The prescribed functions vary enormously, and in literary translation the status of the source text is normally different from that of an advertisement or a legal contract — but the problem as such remains and will be discussed below (see 4.1).

Proceeding from the notion of the text as an integral part of a sociocultural background and stressing the vital importance of the function of a translation, Hönig and Kussmaul then derive their basic criterion for assessing the quality of a translation, their "necessary degree of precision", which represents the point where the function of the target text and decisive sociocultural factors intersect (1982:53). To illustrate this they quote two sentences, each naming a famous British public school:

> In Parliament he fought for equality, but he sent his son to Winchester.

> When his father died his mother couldn't afford to send him to Eton any more.

They then quote two extreme types of translation, with which an experienced translation teacher will be all too familiar:

> ...seinen eigenen Sohn schickte er auf die Schule in Winchester (he sent his own son to the school in Winchester).

> ...konnte es sich seine Mutter nicht mehr leisten, ihn nach Eton zu schicken, jene teure englische Privatschule, aus deren absolventen auch heute noch ein Großteil des politischen und wirtschaftlichen Führungsnachwuchses hervorgeht

> (his mother couldn't afford to send him to Eton, that expensive private school which still produces most of the elite in politics and business.) (1982:58)

The first translation is underdifferentiated: the mere name "Winchester" does not carry the same meaning for a German reader as for the English one. The second translation is overdifferentiated: however correct the information on British public schools may be, it is superfluous for the text concerned. As the necessary grade of differentiation for the texts in question, the authors suggest:

> Im Parlament Kämpfte er für die Chancengleichheit, aber seinen eigenen Sohn schickte er auf eine der englischen Eliteschulen (one of the exclusive English schools).

> Als sein Vater starb, konnte seine Mutter es sich nicht mehr leisten, ihn auf eine der teuren Privatschulen zu schicken (one of the expensive private schools).

This approach rejects the criterion for quality in translation that is still usual in university departments, including translator training institutes, that the translation should "preserve as much of the original as possible" — the classical tenet of equivalence and the main reason why sceptics like Croce and Ortega y Gasset declared that translation was an impossible undertaking. Hönig and Kussmaul present as their criterion, not a global "as much as possible," but a specific "as much as necessary for the function of the text." In other words, we are far from the idea of merely translating words, round which the various translation theories revolved for far too long: the focus is here on the text and — where necessary — on the concept of "words-in-text."

As a cohesive approach to problems of translation, Hönig and Kussmaul's model was new. It was however based on a number of individual concepts already in existence in translation theory, including those of

Funktionskonstanz and *Funktionsveränderung*, as discussed in a number of essays by Vermeer (collected in Vermeer 1983). Hans J. Vermeer has for many years been one of the leading figures in German translation theory: his basic concept is presented in the first part of the book *Grundlegung einer allgemeinen Translationstheorie* (Reiss and Vermeer 1984). Like that of Hönig and Kussmaul, the theory is based on the function of the translated text and is hence called the "Skopostheorie" (Gk. skopos: aim, target).

Vermeer has for many years vehemently opposed the view that translation is simply a matter of language: for him translation is primarily a cross-cultural transfer (see Vermeer 1986), and in his view the translator should be bicultural, if not pluricultural, which naturally involves a command of various languages, as language is an intrinsic part of culture. Secondly, Vermeer views translation as action, als "Sondersorte von Handeln" (1986:36), in other words, it is a "cross-cultural event." This applies to language-pairs that are culturally closely related (like English and German) as well as to language-pairs with only distant cultural connections (such as Finnish and Chinese): the difference is one of degree and not of kind. Vermeer formulates his definition of translation as follows:[4]

> I have defined translation as information offered in a language z of culture Z which imitates information offered in language a of culture A so as to fulfil the desired function. That means that a translation is not the trans-coding of words or sentences from one language into another, but a complex action in which someone provides information about a text under new functional, cultural and linguistic conditions and in a new situation, whereby formal characteristics are imitated as far as possible (1986:36, my translation)

In the *Skopostheorie* the functional element is dominant: "Die Dominante aller Translation ist deren Zweck" (Reiss and Vermeer 1984:96). This Vermeer opposes to the static and absolute attitude to text and translation which debates on what a text "is"; his approach is relative to the individual situation and hence dynamic.

> An advertising text for example cannot be said to "be an advertisement" in absolute terms but is only produced, read or translated as such, everything depending on and varying with the aim of the translation.
> (Reiß and Vermeer 1984:29, my translation)

If Hönig and Kussmaul concentrated on examples of "words-in-text," Vermeer focusses primarily on "text-in-situation,"[5] and this seen holistically against the culture in which it is embedded.

This involves what Vermeer calls the "dethroning of the source text", which for the translator becomes a "means to a new text" (Vermeer, personal communication).[6] This tenet he applies basically to non-literary translation, although the relation of source text to target text varies according to type and function of the translation (see 4.1 below).

Vermeer frequently links his ideas to those of Justa Holz-Mänttäri who, after many years of teaching experience in a Finnish translation college, presented her own theory of translation, *Translatorisches Handeln. Theorie und Methode* (Translatorial Action. Theory and Method) in 1984. The basic approach is very similar to those discussed above, but Holz-Mänttäri is more radical in her methods and conceptual model. As the title of her book indicates, she too views translation, not as a mere transcoding process, but as a form of action across cultures — a cross-cultural event. She even goes as far as to reject the concept of "text," and replaces it with the concept of "message" (*Botschaft*), of which the text is the vehicle (*Botschaftsträger*). Her "translatorisches Handeln" is not a mere act of transferring but a whole complex of actions (*Handlungsgefüge*) involving team-work among experts, from the client to the recipient, whereby the translator plays his own role as expert. Here too translation is seen as an act of *communication* across *cultural barriers*, the main criteria being determined by the *recipient* of the translation and its *specific function*.

What is remarkable about Holz-Mänttäri's approach is her profile of the professional translator as expert (*Professionalisierung*). She explicitly rejects the popular image of the translator as the man (or woman) in the street who buys a bilingual dictionary and attempts to transcode texts as in practical classes at school or university (1986:371, see too Snell-Hornby 1986:9ff.). Her translator is a highly trained and experienced expert, and the same demand is made of those who teach in the training institutions (*Translatologen*).

On first sight Holz-Mänttäri may strike someone deeply entrenched in a humanistic university tradition as being a little exaggerated. In actual fact the complex actions and processes she describes correlate remarkably with the reality of the professional translator's work and requirements, as I can confirm from personal experience in the field (see 4.2 below). Her approach is also attractive to a number of practising translators, who usually tend to be sceptical of any kind of theorizing.[7] One is Hans-Jürgen Stellbrink, head of the language and translating department in a large industrial concern, who rejects both the traditional approach and the linguistically oriented translation theories as being not only useless but even misleading for the future professional translator. In a series of lectures (e.g.

Stellbrink 1984, 1985), he describes the real situation of the translator working in industry, who works essentially as a member of a team, the ultimate aim of his activity lying outside the immediate aim of the translation. The translator of a legal contract, for example, has to aim — beyond the mere working of the text — at providing the necessary legal conditions for international transactions to function, and for this he should assume the full responsibility. The universities — and here Stellbrink is referring to the institutes for translator training — have as yet failed miserably in this concern. He sums up the situation as follows:

> In a seminar on translation theory students shouldn't be familiarized with the various ways of translating "it" into Gaelic — what they should learn is that translation is merely a link in a chain leading to a final goal, and the aim is not the translation, but achieving this goal. (1985:26, my translation)

Once again, this pronouncement should not be taken as a final and absolute judgement on all kinds of translation, and here too the perspective will need to be shifted to account for literary translation. As a starting point however, Stellbrink's words are for the traditionalist a healthy shock of the kind urgently needed to revise diehard and misguided views on the nature of translation.

2.3 System, norm and text

The notion that language is not merely a static inventory of items and rules but a multi-facetted and structured complex was articulated, as we have seen above (2.1), by Humboldt in his theory of the "inner" and "outer" form in language. The same idea was fundamental in the teachings of Saussure, who developed a number of similar concepts known as the "Saussurean dichotomies," and these formed the corner-stone of the structuralist movement which dominated linguistics and even influenced literary studies for decades. The dichotomy we are concerned with here is not the Humboldtian concept developed by Saussure into *signifiant* and *signifié*, but the one which is still central to linguistic studies and is vital for translation theory: the distinction between *langue*, as the abstract language system, and *parole*, as the concrete utterance or text.[8] For a long time linguistics clung to the idea that it is "the *langue*, the language-system, which the linguist describes" (Lyons 1968: 52), and that real life utterances were imperfect or individualistic reflections of the system with inexplicable quirks and deviations that made them unfit for scientific study. It was this attitude that deepened the rift between linguistics and literary studies and accounted for the absurdly simplistic sentences of the type "John hit the ball" used in generative grammar, where no less than 90% of real-life language was excluded as being "deviant" (Lakoff 1982). Translation, as an activity concerned with texts, was naturally excluded from the above-mentioned school of linguistic study. With the fundamental changes that took place in the 1970s however, linguists began to reconsider the relationship between real-life language, language-system and translation theory, and now demands are being made again for what twenty years ago would have been an intrinsic contradiction, for a "linguistique de la parole" — not however in the original structuralist sense (cf. Godel 1981), but with specific orientation towards translation studies (see Schmid 1986:383).

The question is however permitted as to whether the dichotomy of *langue* and *parole* is in itself felicitous. This matter was debated back in the 1930s by the pragmatically oriented British linguist J.R. Firth, who rejected the Saussurean dichotomies outright as being academic constructs incompatible with the realities of language (cf. Firth 1957 and 1968). In a study that appeared in 1951 under the title "Sistema, norma y habla (System, norm and speech)," the question was taken up again by Coseriu (German translation "System, Norm und Rede," Coseriu 1970) who found Saussure's dichotomy inadequate and added the further concept of *norm*. Coseriu's study is in itself embedded in the structuralist principles of its day, and it would be irrelevant to discuss it in detail here. I shall however take up the basic ideas and apply them to our concept of translation. Above all, the polarized dichotomy is once again resolved into a spectrum or cline, with the abstract concept of *system* at the one end and the concrete reality of *text* at the other. Between these two outer areas there is the language prototype or unmarked *norm*.[9] As with Coseriu, the system is here seen as an abstract complex of possibilities: on the grammatical level striking examples would be tense and aspect (these being basically different in English, German and Russian), forms of address (*you* in English as against differentiated forms in other languages), the article (in German expressing gender, number and case versus only reference function in English and zero forms in Slavonic languages) and the varying possibilities of word-formation; examples on the lexical level would be the concepts of semantic fields and paradigms. Unlike Coseriu however, I do not see the norm as being entirely prescriptive: for translation it is at the same time a matter of *prototype* and *convention*. The grammatical norm, as the "grammar rule," is more prescriptive than the lexical norm: the dictionary definition is now seen to embody prototypical usage (cf. Hanks 1985 and 1988, also 1.3 above and 3.5.1 below), whereas convention provides the criteria for relating norms to situations (as with newspaper headlines, 3.3 below).

Norms apply not only in language but at all levels of our social life, and it varies from one community — or culture — to another how "prescriptive" the rules are, how binding the conventions. To illustrate the interplay of rule (norm) and performance (text), Vermeer has used the analogy of the game and the various "rules of the game" (Reiss and Vermeer 1984:97). This same analogy was also a pivotal concept in the hermeneutic approach to translation (see Gadamer 1960; Paepcke 1981 and Forget 1981), where the "rules of the game" — these being both social and language norms — are by no means seen to be as cramping and restrictive as in Coseriu's approach (1951). The rules (or conventions or norms) must indeed be known and observed (cf. Göhring's definition of culture quoted under 2.1 above), but they also provide — as any football fan knows (cf. Forget's comparison in Forget 1981) — *infinite creative potential*. And it is the *controlled use* of this creative potential within language, the tantalizing and unending variety of relationships that exist between rule, norm and the more or less idiosyncratic realization within the possibilities of the system, that provide the point of contact, not only between norm and text, but also between literary and "ordinary" language (see Levý 1969: 82ff., and cf. 4.1 and 4.2 below).

Until recently linguistics viewed the norm as a rigid and prescriptive line of demarcation. In this approach, literary language was simply considered to be deviant: the creative writer moved in a world beyond all objectivity. The concept of the norm was particularly narrow and its prescribed limits correspondingly rigid in transformational grammar, where even lexicalized metaphor was designated as "deviant language" because it did not adhere to the rules of selection restrictions. It is hardly surprising that such an attitude, which dismisses a large area of language as being outside the boundaries of linguistic description, soon found its critics, for whom Uriel Weinreich's celebrated verdict may be quoted as representative: "... a semantic theory is of marginal interest if it is incapable of dealing with poetic uses of language" (1966:471).

Such an approach lays the foundation for what is central to this study: the removal of the still rigid division between literary and "other" language in general, and between literary and "other" translation in particular. As Vermeer points out (1986:35), the difference is one of degree and not of kind. Here too we are dealing, not with a polarized dichotomy, but with a spectrum that admits blends and overlappings. As was pointed out above (1.3.2), even special languages are characterized by metaphor, and journalistic language abounds in "literary" devices such as alliteration and word-play. It is all a question of *quality* and *intensity*, not one of a basic difference.

This means that a number of linguistic dogmas need to be rethought. Here again, some pioneer work was carried out by Coseriu in a short essay "Thesen zum Thema Sprache und Dichtung" (Hypotheses on language and poetry) (1971). Here he states categorically that poetry is not "deviance" from some other kind of language, but the very epitome of language, the realization of all language potential (1971: 185). Against that Coseriu sees ordinary language as representing a reduction of the total language potential. This is very similar to the view held in the present study: literary — and in particular poetic — language is concerned with the *exploitation of the entire capacity of a language system*, in the sense of the game-analogy described above, and involves — not merely deviance from a static and prescriptive norm — but the *creative extension* of the language norm, in the flexible sense of rule-governed potential. As regards translation (see D(i) of the diagram under 1.4 above), this is of fundamental importance: One of the literary translator's most difficult choices is deciding how such creative extensions of the source-language norm can be rendered in the target language without actually infringing the rules of linguistic acceptability.

2.4 Dimension and perspective

Having established the interplay between system, norm and text, I should like to turn to the two broad complementary concepts of *dimension* and *perspective* in their relation to the text. In this sense, *dimension* refers to the linguistic orientation realized in lexical items, stylistic devices and syntactic structures,[10] and it becomes a translation problem when *multidimensionality* in linguistic expression is involved. This not only concerns the interplay of syntax, semantics and pragmatics, but extends to the multiple levels of shifting focus as in metaphors and puns (or any play on words).[11] With *perspective* I mean the viewpoint of the speaker, narrator or reader in terms of culture, attitude, time and place; this shifts, for example, in parody and satire, and invariably in translation. Thus dimension focusses on internal aspects of language, perspective on the relationship of the text to external, social and cultural factors, but again we are not concerned with a dichotomy, but with complementary and often overlapping facets of an integrated whole.[12] If a comparison with a non-linguistic entity is allowed, then I would compare the text, as the terms *dimension* and *perspective* both suggest, to a photograph or film sequence, whereby the individual items gain prominence according to the focussing of the camera and in their relationship to their surroundings.[13]

Word-play provides a particularly striking example of the problems involved. The translation strategy lies in identifying and recreating multiple relationships in both cultural association (perspective) and language (dimension), both at the semantic and the phonological level. A good example of a translation that consciously and in general successfully recreates such relationships is Christian Enzenberger's rendering of *Alice in Wonderland*, as shown in the following extract from the Mock Turtle's famous list of the subjects taken in the school at the bottom of the sea:

> "*Reeling* and *Writhing*, of course, to begin with," the Mock Turtle replied; "and then the different branches of Arithmetic — *Ambition, Distraction, Uglification* and *Derision*." (123)

The dimensions relevant for the translator's analysis are these:

(1) the *semantic congruence* of the two verbs *reel* and *writhe* with a supple agent in constant motion, as befits creatures under water,

(2) the *associations* by *phonological affinity* (*Reeling, Writhing*) with the traditional first subjects of English schoolchildren — the "three Rs," Reading, Writing and Arithmetic — whereby the last item remains constant, the other two vary by one consonant only,

(3) the *phonological affinity* of the four Hard Words *Ambition, Distraction, Uglification* and *Derision* with *Addition, Subtraction, Multiplication* and *Division*, the degree of variation differing from one case to another,

(4) the *negative connotations* of *Derision* and the coinage *Uglification*, which both reflect the Mock Turtle's sorrowful mode of discourse and reproduce the didactic severity inherent in the dialogue concerned.

Enzensberger recreates this web of relationships to appeal specifically to the German reader of the mid-20th century in his own cultural sphere:[14]

"Also, zunächst einmal das große und das Kleine *Nabelweh*, natürlich," antwortete die Falsche Suppenschildkröte, aber dann auch Deutsch und alle Unterarten — *Schönschweifen, Rechtspeibung, Sprachelbeere* und *Hausversatz*. (1963:99)

Observing that the "three Rs" have been resolved into "das Große und das Kleine Abc" and "Deutsch," we can analyze the dimensions of this German text as follows:

(1) the basic *formal pattern of constants and variables* has been preserved,

(2) the Hard Words have been replaced by *morphologically transparent compounds*, all of them newly coined: 'Schönschweifen' for *Schönschreiben*, 'Rechtspeibung' for *Rechtsschreibung*, 'Sprachelbeere' for *Sprachlehre* and 'Hausversatz' for *Hausaufsatz*, thus reproducing by association the four basic components of elementary instruction in the subject "Deutsch" in German schools,

(3) beside the *negative connotations* we have an additional element of *parody* provided by the association with *Stachelbeere* (in 'Sprachelbeere'), which then (on *analogy* with 'uglify' and *beautify* in the English text) is developed into a sequence of further puns on diverse fruits, such as 'Erdbeerkunde' (against 'Seaography' in the English original, p.124).

The concept of dimension as used here thus concerns the relationships observable between linguistic structures and devices in the text; in the above example these were *semantic congruence*, associations by *phonological affinity* and *morphological formations* as well as *connotations*.[15] The last element, in its relation to the sociocultural background on the one hand and to parodic imitation on the other, links up with our second concept of perspective, which, like dimension, involves a dynamic system of shifting relationships, in this case however extending beyond the text to its immediate situation and its cultural background. Perspective need not be a translation problem where the cultural background is distant and exotic for both source-language and target-language reader, but it presents real difficulties where the reader of the source-language text is appealed to as a member of a particular cultural or social group, and where knowledge of or even a relationship to this culture is presupposed — here the question of perspective will clearly affect the reception of the translated work.[16]

A positive explosion of perspectives can be found in the plays of Tom Stoppard, presenting myriad problems for the translator (cf. Snell-Hornby 1984). The following is a relatively simple passage from Stoppard's academic satire *Jumpers*, and with the satirical component the basic perspective of the play has already been set. These lines are part of an academic paper on fundamental problems of existence as dictated to a secretary by George Moore, Professor of Moral Philosophy:

> Consider my left sock. My left sock exists but it need not have done so. It is, we say, not necessary but contingent. Why does my sock exist? Because a sock-maker made it, in one sense; because, in another, at some point previously, the conception of a sock arrived in the human brain; to keep my foot warm in a third, to make a profit in a fourth. There is reason and there is cause and there is the question, who made the sock-maker's maker. (Act I, p.28)

On the purely linguistic level, the text would seem to present no problems for any translator with even average proficiency in English. Precisely for this reason it provides excellent evidence for Vermeer's requirement that a translator should not only be bilingual, but above all bicultural: only someone with a good knowledge of the specific cultural background concerned is able to identify the complexities of perspective that have to be dealt with. Firstly, the translator must recognize that the passage parodies the kind of language associated with the British philosophy professor, whereby existential problems are pondered earnestly on the basis of everyday examples;[17] anyone translating the text into German would have to know that such associations are not made with German philosophers. A second problem involves both perspective and dimension: the passage gains depth by the allusion to the famous comparison with the clock(maker), heightened by the phonological affinity of *clock* and *sock*, which is lost in the equivalent comparison with the *Uhr(macher)*. It is in fact the item *sock* which lends the passage its parodic perspective of apparent triviality: if *sock* were replaced throughout by *clock* (with corresponding adjuncts and attributes), these lines could well constitute serious-minded reflections familiar in the British tradition.

Let us now look at the authorized German translation by Hilde Spiel:

> Betrachten Sie meine linke Socke. Meine linke Socke existiert, aber eigentlich müßte sie das gar nicht. Es ist, wie wir sagen, nicht notwendig, sondern zufällig. Warum existiert meine Socke? In einem Sinn, weil ein Sockenmacher sie gemacht hat, in einem anderen Sinn, weil sich zu irgendeinem früheren Zeitpunkt der Begriff Socke im menschlichen Gehirn

gebildet hat, in einem dritten, um meinen Fuß warmzuhalten, in einem
vierten, um einen Gewinn zu erzielen. Es gibt die Vernunft und es gibt das
Kausalprinzip und es gibt die Frage, wer hat den gemacht, der den Socken-
macher machte?

This literal transcoding of the passage reduces the text to a level of trivial
banality; the perspective of parodic imitation disappears entirely, although
the language of German philosophy shows marked characteristics which
would lend themselves to such treatment. What disappears too is the credi-
bility of the German stage-character: in the opinion of translation experts
discussing this passage, the English George Moore is recognizable through
the parody as an academic, while his German counterpart comes across as
"ein Depp" (a twit).[18]

2.4.1 *The translation of metaphor*

Scholars agree that metaphor has been sadly neglected in translation
theory. In the standard works of the linguistically oriented schools (Nida
1964; Nida and Taber 1969; Reiss 1971; Wilss 1977; Koller 1979) the topic is
barely discussed, and in Mounin's classic study (1967) it is not even mentioned. The subject was taken up by Menachim Dagut in 1976 in an essay
entitled "Can 'Metaphor' be translated?," a further essay "The limits of
translatability exemplified by metaphor translation" by Raymond van den
Broeck appeared in 1981, while Newmark devoted a chapter of his pragmatically and linguistically oriented book *Approaches to Translation* (1981)
to the issue "The translation of metaphor."[19]

It is not the aim of this chapter to expound the — partially conflicting
— views expressed in the above articles, nor can I attempt even a brief survey of the vast amount of material that has appeared on metaphor in literary studies (cf. Shibles 1970 and Van Noppen et al. 1985). I would like to
concentrate here on metaphor as a translation problem in the light of the
integrated approach favoured in this study, in particular as regards the
phenomena of dimension and perspective. Reference will however be made
to the three articles mentioned above where they are relevant for our
approach.

Of basic importance in our approach is the conviction that *metaphor is
text* (Weinrich 1976). Thus the concept of the "one-word metaphor" (Newmark 1981:85) is rejected. As an example of the postulated "one-word
metaphor," Newmark cites the phrase "a *sunny* girl"; the metaphor does

not however lie only in the one word *sunny*, but in the *impact* of *sunny* and *girl*, hence in the combination of what Newmark has named for translation purposes the *object* or the item described by the metaphor (here *girl*), the *image*, or item in terms of which the metaphor is described (in Richards' classic terminology the "vehicle," here "sun"), and the *sense* (the "tenor" in Richards' terminology), or the traditional tertium comparationis, which shows in what particular aspects the object and the image are similar. Thus in the metaphorical phrase "a sunny girl," the sense lies in the implicit elements "bright, cheerful, happy," and the metaphor — far from being only one word — is a complex of *three dimensions*. The essential problem posed by metaphor in translation is that different cultures, hence different languages, conceptualize and create symbols in varying ways, and therefore the sense of the metaphor is frequently culture-specific. Such is the case with metaphors involving animals, as in the one also quoted by Newmark "She is a cat,"[20] where the sense can be identified as "spiteful, malicious." In German however a "Katze" is not associated with spitefulness or malice but with grace and agility, and a literal transcoding of the English sentence would not communicate the metaphorical meaning. Conversely, the statement frequently heard in German to express a similar sentiments as the English, "Sie ist eine alte Ziege" (old goat), expresses a blend of stupidity and unpleasantness associated with neither *goat* nor *cat*. And that this is primarily a matter of culture and not language system is shown by the fact that in American Black English "cat" may be used of both men and women merely to indicate "person" without pejorative associations.

A metaphor is then a complex of (at least) three dimensions, reflecting the tension between resemblance and disparity, whereby, as Newmark aptly puts it, a new truth is created that requires a "suspension of disbelief, a fusion of perception and imagination" (1985:296). How "new" this truth really is varies greatly with the metaphor concerned. Various typologies of metaphor have been offered, including those of Dagut, Newmark and Van den Broeck: they are all box-like categories of the classical school and are open to criticism. What most metaphor typologies seem to have in common however, is the polarization of "original" metaphors on the one hand and "dead" metaphors on the other, with a broad and disputed territory lying in between. This is the concept in keeping with our approach, and which I should like to develop here in its relevance for translation.

The "dead" metaphor is generally accepted as being one no longer recognizable as such: in his discussion of the topic, Leech (1974:228) quotes *thrill* as an example, which in Old English (*thyrlian*) had the meaning "to pierce." At the other end of the scale is the "original" or "individual" metaphor as presented by Shakespeare or Dickens. Between them lies a broad spectrum of what Bolinger has described in evocative terms as "faded" metaphors: "A dictionary is a frozen pantomime. Our problem is only beginning when we consider the pale flowers of that 'nosegay of faded metaphors' that it presses between its pages." (1965:567) The relation of dictionary and word will be discussed below (3.5), but Bolinger's mention of the dictionary shows that the "fading" of a metaphor is a gradual process of lexicalization from the familiar quote that forms part of a cultural heritage (Hamlet's "sea of troubles" or Homer's "rosy-finger'd dawn"), via the familiar phrase no longer recognized as a quotation and the "figurative sense" found in the dictionary to the technical term (such as *dumping* or *boom* in the economic sense) which gradually loses the concrete denotation it once had. Precisely where a metaphor is situated on this scale cannot be determined by a system of watertight categories: its position shifts with cultural developments, and whether a quotation is recognized or a double sense perceived often depends on the knowledge and experience of the individual.

A question which has interested the few translation theorists who have discussed metaphor is which kind of metaphor is the easiest to translate. Kloepfer (1967), in discussing a German translation of Rimbaud's "Metropolitain" by W. Küchler, makes the following sweeping statements:

> Küchler manages to preserve all the metaphors: their famous "boldness" is no problem for the translation — on the contrary, the bolder and more creative the metaphor, the easier it is to repeat it in other languages. There is not only a "harmony of metaphorical fields" among the various European languages, there are concrete metaphorical fields common to all mankind, but there are also definite "structures of the imagination" on which they are based. (1976:116, my translation)

These statements were severely criticized by Dagut, along with the views of Reiss on translating metaphor (quoted in 1.3.2 above), and in particular her recommendation that an original metaphor should be translated literally (1971:62f.). Dagut places this "no problem" approach in contrast to the frequently postulated "untranslatability" of metaphor (especially in poetry) and, on the basis of an analysis of some Hebrew texts and their English translations, he concludes that the problem in translating metaphor vary considerably:

> ... the translatability of any given SL metaphor depends on (1) the particular *cultural experiences and semantic associations* exploited by it, and (2) the extent to which these can, or cannot, be reproduced non-anomalously

in TL, depending on the *degree of "overlap" in each particular case.*
(1976:32, emphasis added)

These observations harmonize with the approach adopted here, and I
would endorse both Dagut's final conclusions and his rejection of the
simplistic generalizations made in Kloepfer 1967 and Reiss 1971. Whether
a metaphor is "translatable" (i.e. whether a literal translation could
recreate identical dimensions), how difficult it is to translate, how it can
be translated and whether it should be translated at all cannot be decided
by a set of abstract rules, but must depend on the structure and function
of the particular metaphor within the text concerned.

I would like to illustrate this by three examples, the first two taken
from an article in the *Neue Zürcher Zeitung* (7.4.1978) and reproduced on
the following page with their relevant textual background. The passage concerned is the first paragraph of an essay describing visual impressions of
Belfast in 1978, with the perspective of a Swiss journalist and as compared
with a previous visit before hostilities started: The title could be rendered
"Belfast Revisited." The subtitle "Trostloses Meer verrusster Häuser-
reihen" contains a metaphor that is taken up again and expanded in the
body of the text (lines 9-11). The image "trostloses Meer" expresses above
all what the writer experiences as endless monotony, but on the metaphorical level it is by no means equivalent to English *sea*, which as a lexicalized
metaphor implies potential movement, as for example in the phrase "a sea
of faces."[21] What is being described in the German text is a rigid, static
impression of zigzag roofs,[22] for which *sea* ("a sea of roofs?") would be an
incongruous image. In such cases it is up to the translator to decide whether
the metaphorical image is vital for the text and whether it contributes
towards the general understanding of the text, and if so, in how far the
image must be adapted to the target culture. In the present case the image
has no further function in the text and is superfluous for the general understanding of the message, and while it might add a certain atmospheric
undertone, it makes no real aesthetic contribution to the description of Belfast; with "dreary view" the altogether rather banal German metaphor is
quite adequately rendered. This is not infrequently the case with metaphor
used in journalistic texts, but quite independently of text-typology, the
above example illustrates what Newmark aptly calls the translator's "dis-
criminating sense of priority," "what he thinks more important and less
important in the text in relation to its intention," and it shows effectively
how the translator "has to assess the status of the metaphor before he

Neue Zürcher Zeitung

4   Freitag, 7. April 1978   Nr. 80

Wiedersehen mit Belfast

Trostloses Meer verrusster Häuserreihen

Von unserem Korrespondenten Roger Bernheim

Belfast, 5. April

Selbst unter günstigsten Umständen ist Belfast kein attraktiver Ort, und günstige Umstände herrschen hier schon seit neun Jahren nicht mehr. Die Stadt ist ein *Produkt der industriellen Revo-*
5 *lution* im letzten Jahrhundert, eilig aufgebaut für Unternehmer und Arbeiter: Fabriken, Schiffswerften, Handelskontore und endlose Häuserzeilen für Arbeiterwohnungen, jede Zeile identisch mit der andern — ein trostloses Meer aus dunkel-
10 rotbraunen Ziegelsteinen, aus dem verrusste Schlote emporragen. Erst gegen die Hänge der umliegenden Hügel hin und weiter gegen die Küste zu, wo die Bessergestellten ihre Häuser gebaut haben, hellt sich das Stadtbild auf. Die
15 Hauptstrassen, die   / vom Zentrum ausgehen, teilen die Stadt in Kreissektoren auf, die in abwechselnder Folge von Katholiken und Protestanten bewohnt sind, so dass jede Gruppe sich immer von beiden Seiten her bedroht fühlt.

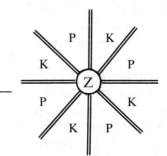

translates." (1985: 323)

The second example in the same passage illustrates quite a different problem: the underlined sentence (lines 14-19), contains an (obliterated) simile essential for the understanding of the text and hence crucial for the translation. In the diagram to the right of the extract I have reproduced the information encoded in this sentence, particularly as expressed by the obliterated simile. The sentence (minus simile) could be rendered in English as follows, the letters in brackets referring to the diagram:

> The main streets, which lead from the centre (Z) (simile), divide the city into districts alternately inhabited by Catholics (K) and Protestants (P), so that each group always feels threatened from both sides.

In order to show up the difference in metaphorical association even between two so closely related languages as English and German, I first asked native speakers of English to tell me what they thought the drawing represented, hence what they thought the simile could be, and then I asked some native speakers of German to replace the missing word in the text. Both groups answered without hesitation, and almost unanimously: the Germans identified the missing word correctly as *strahlenförmig*, and the English native speakers saw in the lines of the diagram "the spokes of a wheel."[23] Of over 150 students who translated the text however, the over-whelming majority rendered *strahlenförmig* either with "like rays of the sun" or with "like rays of a star."[24] This illustrates the "equivalence syndrome" (cf. 1.2.3 above), that immediate impulse typical of the untrained student to look for an "equivalent" lexical unit in the target language without relating it to the text. In English the image "rays of the sun" evokes a visual impression of diffuse emitted light; what is essential to this text however is to depict the sharp divisions between the various districts of Belfast, a function adequately fulfilled by the German image *Strahl*, a lexeme semantically not identical to English *ray*. Such sharp delineation would be implied in the image "spokes of a wheel," which is however essentially static and thus incongruous with the dynamic element expressed in the German verb *ausgehen*. A better solution would be to replace the simile by the metaphorical verb *radiate* (which both preserves the dynamic, centre-oriented element and implies the visual image of light) and leave the semantic function of expressing sharp delineation to the reinforcing verb *divide*. Thus the English translation could run: "The main streets, radiating from the city centre, divide the town into districts...."

My third example is an original metaphor, also visual in nature and also nominal in linguistic form; it is taken from an intensely descriptive passage in Thomas Mann's story *Das Wunderkind*. The German sentence runs as follows (the metaphor concerned is italicized):

> Es ist ein prunkhafter Saal, gelegen in einem modischen Gasthof ersten Ranges, mit rosig fleischlichen Gemälden an den Wänden, mit üppigen Pfeilern, umschnörkelten Spiegeln und einer Unzahl, *einem wahren Weltensystem von elektrischen Glühlampen*, die in Dolden, in ganzen Bündeln überall hervorsprießen und den Raum mit einem weit übertaghellen, dünnen, goldigen, himmlischen Licht durchzittern. (52)

Concentrating on the image "einem wahren Weltensystem von elektrischen Glühlampen," let us now compare the English translation by Helen Lowe-Porter:

> Ornamental columns supported a ceiling that displayed *a whole universe of electric bulbs*, in clusters darting a brilliance far brighter than day and filling the whole space with thin, vibrating golden light. (175)

In reproducing the metaphor, this translator has also succumbed to the* habit of hunting for dictionary equivalents without adequately considering the function and relevance of the metaphor to the text. The two elements essential to the metaphor are, firstly, the *visual* impression of light, and secondly, the effect of what is described as a *vast number* of individual lights. Neither element is adequately rendered in *universe* or *bulbs*: the sense of the metaphor "universe" would be a totality, whether envisaged as a concrete mass or an abstract whole, whereas the sense of *Weltensystem* in the German text rather evokes a *galaxy* of stars; furthermore, *bulb* — with reference to *Glühlampe* — focusses not so much on the light emitted as on the electrical applicance itself (hence *Glühbirne*), whether it is burning or not. In all, both the general sense of the metaphor and its aesthetic appeal have been inadequately rendered: more justice would have been done to it in a phrase like "a veritable galaxy of electric lights."[25]

Some interesting points emerge from these examples. Besides the subtle shifts in imagery and association that occur in translation, both the newspaper item and the literary text illustrate the already discussed interplay between system, (language) norm and text. A striking example is *strahlenförmig* as against *radiate*. Firstly, while the German language system favours the formation of such morphologically transparent compounds (see too *übertaghell* and *durchzittern* as creative formations in the literary text), the English language system tends to favour the formation of morphologically opaque Hard Words of Latin or Greek origin. Secondly, whereas in German adverbial phrases tend to take the semantic load of a sentence (as in this case), English stresses the verb phrase (as in the translation). While *strahlenförmig* represents an "unmarked norm" lexicalized in the language, Mann's formation *übertaghell* represents a creative extension of the norm made possible by the creative potential in the same language system.

The second point that must be stressed yet again is the dependence of language on culture as demonstrated by metaphor. In the theoretical discussion we were once again confronted with the views of the "universal" school (as postulated in Kloepfer's "metaphorical fields common to all mankind"), which insists that all metaphor is translatable, as against the opposed view of the absolute "untranslatability" of metaphor (as in poetry). These examples indicate that the answer lies somewhere between the two poles, depending on the structure and function of the metaphor within the text. As an abstract concept, metaphor might be universal (as

claimed in Newmark 1981); in its concrete realization however, being
closely linked with sensuous perception and culture-bound value judge-
ments, it is undoubtedly complicated by language-specific idiosyncracies.
And therein lies its fascination for the translator.

Notes

1. It is important to note that Göhring's definition was conceived expressly in the *contrastive* sense and as a basis for translation studies. See too Oksaar 1988.

2. This correlates precisely with Fillmore's conception of *scene* in his scenes-and-frames semantics (see Chapter 3.3).

3. The principle studies used in Hönig and Kussmaul's discussion are: Stein 1980; Crystal and Davy 1969; Searle 1969; Hörmann 1976 and Quirk and Greenbaum 1973. As is often the case in translation studies, these studies are not used to develop a linguistic discussion as such, but as a basis from which to derive ideas on translation theory.

4. The definition presented here is a summary of previous definitions presented in Vermeer 1983.

5. The term "Text-in-Situation" was coined by Vermeer for specific use in translation studies (see Vermeer 1983).

6. These are phrases used by Vermeer in the discussion following his lecture "Zur Begrün- dung von Übersetzungsvarianten. Warum es *die* Übersetzung nicht gibt" (In defence of translation variants. Why *the* (perfect) translation does not exist) held at the University of Zurich on 21.5.1984. Vermeer 1986 is based on this lecture.

7. Hönig and Kussmaul sum up the situation very aptly as follows: "Überspitzt ausgedrückt nähern wir uns heute schon einem Zustand, in dem die Übersetzer die Theorie nicht mehr zur Kenntnis nehmen und die Wissenschaftler keine Erfahrung mit dem praktischen Geschäft des Übersetzens haben. Eine solche Konfrontation: Hier Praktiker — hier Theoretiker, kann beiden Seiten nur schaden." (1982:15) (We are reaching the point where translators take no notice of theory and the theorists have no experience in transla- tion. A confrontation of theorists and practitioners can only do harm to both.)

8. This distinction is similar to Chomsky's dichotomy of *competence* and *performance*, and — especially in English linguistic writings — the two pairs of concepts are often freely interchanged as though they were precisely the same. It is important to point out however that they are not identical: Saussure's dichotomy refers to the phenomenon of language, Chomsky's to the language-*user* as idealized speaker-hearer. In this study the dichotomy is used in the Saussurean sense and in the Saussurean terminology.

9. This term is now standard currency in translation theory, both in the linguistic and cul- tural sense, and is also gaining ground in theoretical work on lexicography (cf. Hanks 1985).

10. The term *linguistic* is used here in its sense "of language" (hence: "of language as a part of culture") and has no reference to the discipline of linguistics.

11. The additional term "play on words" is included to save confusion with *pun* in the strictly Shakespearean sense.

12. On the superficial level this distinction seems similar to Reiss's *innersprachliche Instruktionen* as against *außersprachliche Determinanten* (1971), but basically the conception is quite different: Reiss presents a clear-cut division and on each side a checklist of items, while here we are concerned less with factorizing than with reconstructing the text as a cohesive unit.

13. The first incentive for applying the terms *dimension* and *perspective* to texts first came to me while translating documentary film commentaries, where screen image and spoken text merged into a single unit of visual and acoustic perception. Cf. Snell-Hornby 1984a.

14. This point he states clearly in his *Nachwort* (p. 129).

15. For a discussion of *connotation* see Vermeer 1971: 43, also Snell-Hornby 1983:48.

16. This is not only a problem of literary translation: for a detailed study of the phenomenon of perspective in political speeches (as a specific problem of the conference interpreter) see Merz 1986.

17. The Moral Philosophy Professor J.L. Austin gives some idea of this popular lecturing technique in Austin 1962.

18. This was the view expressed by the Joyce expert Klaus Reichert in the discussion following a presentation of this topic and Stoppard's text with the German translation (Workshop "Die Literarische Übersetzung," Göttingen, October 1985).

19. Van den Broeck 1981 was first presented as a paper in the Symposium "Translation Theory and Intercultural Relations" held at the University of Tel Aviv in 1978. Newmark 1981 first appeared in *Babel* 26, 1980, p.93-100 and then, in revised form, in Newmark 1985. See too Snell-Hornby 1988.

20. Newmark attributes this image to connotation (1981: 85). For a lexicographical discussion of the metaphorical sense of *cat* see Ayto 1988.

21. This is the example given in ALD. Note the CED definition: *Sea* (...) 5. anything resembling the sea in size or apparent limitlessness. COD quotes as figurative examples of *sea*: *A sea of troubles, care, flame, upturned faces.*

22. This can be deduced from (a) the perspective of spatial distance inferred by the metaphor and (b) factual knowledge of the type of houses referred to. Wahrig quotes as figurative examples of *Meer: Ein Meer von Blut, von Tränen; ein unübersehbares Meer von Häusern; ein Meer von Irrtümern, Mißverständnissen; ein Meer von Licht, von Tönen.*

23. As an alternative to *strahlenförmig, sternförmig* was also suggested. Compare Kafka's description of a similar basic lay-out in his novel *Amerika*: "... die großen Plätze, von denen sternförmig die Straßen auseinanderflogen...."
The experiment referred to here was carried out at a Linguistic Workshop in Trier in March 1983; it has been repeated several times since, always with the same result.

24. This is the total number of students from varying translation classes, both in translation training institutes and English Departments.

25. Note CED definitions: *Universe*: 1. the *aggregate* of all existing matter, energy, and space, 2. human beings *collectively* (emphasis added); *galaxy* 1. any of a vast number of star systems held together by gravitational attraction in an asymmetrical shape.

3. Translation, text and language

3.1 Linguistics and translation

> But it is its great untidiness that makes human speech innovative and expressive of personal intent. It is the anomaly, as it feeds back into the general history of usage, the ambiguity, as it enriches and complicates the general standard of definition, which give coherence to the system. A coherence, if such a description is allowed, 'in constant motion.' The vital constancy of that motion accounts for both the epistemological and psychological failure of the project of a 'universal character.' (Steiner 1975:203)

In the longest chapter of his book, entitled "Word against Object" — clearly adapted to contradict Quine's *Word and Object* (1960) — Steiner discusses the tension, the unspeakably complex relation between language and world. In doing so, he pulls apart some of the basic dogmas of some schools of linguistics that were still dominant when he was writing his book: the concept of language universals as propagated by the Chomskyan school, the conception of language as a code as inherited from Saussure and developed in the theories of structuralism, the notion of the sentence as a "string" of items as was fundamental to transformational grammar and — underlying them all — the belief in a static and absolute tertium comparationis, in relation to which universally valid concepts are simply given differing labels in the various languages (the concept of "equivalence" discussed in 1.2.3 above).

If these dogmas were right, translation would indeed be a simple task, a mere "praktische Fertigkeit," as traditionalists are still inclined to describe it, that merely requires learning vocabulary lists and applying grammar rules. Meanwhile this simplistic view has been undermined even within the discipline of linguistics. At this stage it must however be pointed out that there is one exceptional type of translation which both confirms and depends on those dogmas questioned by Steiner, and that is "MT," or machine translation. Machine translation is not the subject of the present study, but if we postulate an integrated approach to translation, we cannot ignore it completely. In the diagram under 1.4 above, MT is represented by items on the extreme right of the spectrum: it coordinates with technological texts, conceptual identity, the purely informational function, and standardized terminology. In other words, its range is extremely limited and depends on some specific external factors, including an identical referential background for both source and target text, and the total absence of any ambiguity in the linguistic items. Within this limited area, MT has had conspicuous success, a frequently cited example being the TAUM-METEO Project for weather forecast programmes (French and English) in Canada (see Gutknecht 1987: 253). Even where it ventures into the complications and ambiguities that characterize most of natural language, machine translation has proved itself worthwhile — but with definite limits. There are the "batch systems" of machine translation that require pre-editing and post-editing plus a reduction of lexis and syntax to a level of simplification that belies the genius of human language.

More recently, new systems of machine translation have been developed, the "interactive systems" (cf. Moser-Mercer 1986), where the human translator — instead of submitting to the machine — guides and controls it in a process of decision-making similar to that in human translation. Even here however, only certain stereotypes texts are possible (technological text, instructions for use, etc.), and the sentence is reduced to a linear string of items, whereby textual cohesion is dependent on the human translator.

By far the most spectacular success, and hence an assured future in the development of translation, can be seen in machine-*aided* translation (MAT), where linguistic items (such as terminological data) are stored in data-banks and made accessible to the human translator (cf. 3.5 below), who is then fully responsible for the syntax and textual cohesion of the target text. This area of translation is at present undergoing an explosive development, and it will have to be given more consideration within the discipline of translation studies than has been the case up to now (cf. Kaiser-Cooke 1993). It is however a far cry from the euphoria of the 1950s, when linguists seriously thought that the machine was embarking on a triumphal march across the territory of translation as a whole (cf. Weaver 1955 and Moser-Mercer 1986); it was Bar-Hillel who in 1960 dampened the optimism, and now there is no longer any doubt that the product of technology, however sophisticated, cannot compete with the creative power of the human mind.

This development is inextricably involved with the changing views within the discipline of linguistics, which up to 1970 was dominated by the "appearance of transformational grammar as a serious candidate for an adequate theory of human language" (Statement of Purpose in the first issue of *Linguistic Inquiry*, 1970:1). A theory covering the phenomenon of human language would naturally involve translation. In recent years however the opinion has gained ground among translation theorists that transformational grammar, and to a certain extent structural linguistics in general, have been detrimental to the development of a general translation theory. This view was stated explicitly by Beaugrande (1978:8), who maintains that such schools of thought provided concepts and procedures totally inappropriate for translation, as for example, their emphasis on the formal classification of constants at the expense of variables, the restriction of study to word and sentence level, and above all, their exclusion of the study of meaning. Catford's "theory of translation" (1965) is eloquently dismissed as an "allegory of the limitations of linguistics at that time" (Beaugrande 1978:11). I would fully endorse Beaugrande's opinion, and find it significant that translation as a subject considered worthy of serious academic study gained impetus with the rise of disciplines such as sociolinguistics and cross-cultural studies, which view language in its infinite variability and in relation to human behaviour and perception, culture and communication.

This development, known in Germany as the "pragmatische Wende" (pragmatic turn), has recently been described by Wilss (1987) in its importance for translation studies. It should however be pointed out that the interaction of translation and language studies need not be merely a matter of chronological development, that there are older developments in linguistics on which translation studies might profitably draw. These approaches all have certain prerequisites in common: firstly, they are based on a worldview which *synthesizes* rather than separates; secondly, they do not view language as an isolated phenomenon, but *relate* it both to the world around and to other disciplines; thirdly, they adhere to culture-bound *differentiation* rather than universalist theories; and fourthly, they work *empirically* and *inductively* with concrete language material.

Two linguists of this kind whose work has influenced translation studies have already been mentioned: Wilhelm von Humboldt and Benjamin Lee Whorf. It is not irrelevant that both distinguished themselves professionally in fields other than language studies: Humboldt as politician and educational reformer, and Whorf as a chemical engineer working for an insurance company. In particular Whorf's observations on language were based as much on practical everyday experience as on the study of exotic tongues.[1]

Another school of linguistics which proved invaluable for translation studies is the so-called Prague Circle, whose founding members (in particular V. Mathesius, R. Jakobson, N. Trubetzkoy, B. Havránek and B. Trnka)[2] represent a spectrum of scholarship ranging from phonology and syntax to literary theory and covering many European languages, including English and German, Czech and Russian. One of the earliest principles of the Prague School was the synthesis of elements from the two apparently conflicting streams of 19th century language study: the synchronic, inductive and holistic approach of the Humboldt school was to be combined with the rigorous scientific method of the Neogrammarians. The result was a blossoming of linguistic scholarship concentrating especially on the contemporary language and which was both structuralist and functional in approach.

A legacy of direct interest to translation was the concept of Functional Sentence Perspective (FSP) with the connected concepts of *theme* and *rheme* (associated especially with the work of F. Daneš and J. Firbas). The notions of theme and rheme as given and new information were to become fundamental in textual analysis (see Halliday 1976; Halliday and Hasan 1976; Beaugrande and Dressler 1981; Scherner 1984 and many others), and along with related notions like thematic progression, focus and stress were to pave the way for new developments in translation studies (as illustrated by both the flexible approach in Hönig and Kussmaul 1982 and the rigorous formal analysis in Gerzymisch-Arbogast 1986).

In general however the most fruitful interaction between linguistics and translation theory came with the pragmatic reorientation of the 1970s or indirectly via other disciplines: via language philosophy with the insights of Wittgenstein and Gadamer, via moral philosophy with the speech act theory of Austin and Searle, via psychology with experiments like those of Rosch, and via sociology in the form of sociolinguistics — as the study of language variety, language behaviour and communication within differing social contexts.

3.2 Text analysis

The preceding chapter (2) was devoted to the interdependence of culture and translation; we are now going to investigate the complex relationship between translation and language-in-text, a kind of dialectic tension which — to borrow from Steiner — might be described as "Word against Text." It is the aim of the following sections to elucidate what is meant by this.

With the development of text-linguistics[3] and the gradual emergence of translation studies as an independent discipline in its own right, there has been an increasing awareness of the text, not as a chain of separate sentences, these themselves a string of grammatical and lexical items (as was the case with the translation unit discussed in 1.2.3 above), but as a complex, multi-dimensional structure consisting of more than the mere sum of its parts — a gestalt, as was explained in 1.3.1 above, whereby an analysis of its parts cannot provide an understanding of the whole. Thus textual analysis, which is an essential preliminary to translation,[4] should proceed from the "top down," from the macro to the micro level, from text to sign.

We have already established too that for the translator the text is not purely a linguistic phenomenon, but must also be seen in terms of its *communicative* function, as a unit embedded in a given *situation*, and as part of a broader sociocultural background (2.2). Taking that as the point of departure, the translator's text analysis should begin by *identifying* the text in terms of culture and situation, as "part of a world-continuum" (Vermeer 1983). The next step is the analysis of the *structure* of the text, proceeding down from the macro-structure to the level of lexical cohesion and including the relationship between the *title* and the main body of the text, and finally *strategies* should be developed for translating the text, based on conclusions reached from the analysis. It is important to stress again that the analysis is not concerned with isolating phenomena or items to study them in depth, but with tracing a *web of relationships*, the importance of individual items being determined by their relevance and function in the text (cf. 1.4 and 2.4.1 above).

The text chosen to illustrate this type of analysis is "The Pacific" by W. Somerset Maugham (1874-1965), an evocative sketch of the varying moods and atmosphere of the Pacific Ocean which introduces the collection of short stories *The Trembling of a Leaf*, published in 1921. This text has been chosen firstly because it is a short, manageable and complete text in itself, and can at the same time be placed in relationship to the stories in the book. Secondly, if not an outstanding work of art, it is of a literary nature and illustrates how this method of analysis extends beyond technical and general language.

At this point it is necessary to clarify what is meant by a literary text. We have established above (2.3) that literary language cannot be dismissed as merely "deviant" language, but on the contrary, as Coseriu (1971) maintained, it rather represents the creative exploitation of the language potential against which ordinary language represents a reduction. This applies of course in varying degrees to the abundance of texts described as literary, and it cannot suffice as a definition of a literary text. As a text-type, the literary text is often, though not quite accurately, equated with fiction; in this study we are adopting the broad definition as suggested by Beaugrande and Dressler: a text that presents a systematic alternative to the accepted version of the "real world" (1981:191). Between the "real world" and the "systematic alternative" there is of course no clear dividing-line, and Beaugrande and Dressler refer to the varying degrees of discrepancy between the textual world and the "real world" (1981:191). Seen in that light, "The Pacific" is on the fringes of the category "literary text" with considerable agreement and overlapping between the "real world" and the world of the text. It is far from being merely a travel report or geographical account however, as clearly emerges from the analysis, though the perspective (see 2.4 above) is that of the writer who knows that part of the world from personal experience and describes it for the European (or even British) reader (see lines 2/3, reference to the "English Channel off Beachy Head") with an implicit appeal for empathy. At the time of publication Maugham was 47 and had been travelling widely all over the world. The theme of the European in alien surroundings and his emotional disintegration in the heady world of the tropics is a familiar one in Maugham's works. In the 1920s, when the British Empire was still flourishing, such far-off tropical zones had a meaning for the educated English reader even outside his personal experience. Hence the title is not merely a geographical name, but is used to evoke associations in the reader's mind.

The title "The Pacific" is immediately taken up as the theme of the first sentence, which itself acts as a *Leitmotiv* for the entire text: the characterization of the Pacific as "inconstant," motivating the comparison with "the

THE PACIFIC (1921)

The Pacific[1] is inconstant[2] and uncertain,[2] like the
soul of man.[2] Sometimes it is grey[3] like the English
Channel[4] off Beachy Head,[4] with a heavy swell,[1] and
sometimes it is rough,[1] capped with white crests,[3] and
5   boisterous.[2] It is not so often that it is calm[1] and blue.[3]
Then, indeed, the blue[3] is arrogant.[2] The sun shines[3]
fiercely[2] from an unclouded sky.[4] The trade wind[4]
gets into your blood[2] and you are filled with an im-
patience[2] for the unknown. The billows, magnificently
10 rolling,[1] stretch widely on all sides of you, and you
forget your vanished youth,[2] with its memories,[2] cruel
and sweet, in a restless, intolerable desire for life.[2]
On such a sea as this[1] Ulysses sailed when he sought the
Happy Isles. // But there are days also when the Pacific
15 is like a lake.[1] The sea[1] is flat and shining.[3] The flying
fish,[4] a gleam of shadow[3] on the brightness[3] of a mirror,[1]
make little fountains[4] of sparkling[3] drops[4] when they dip.[4]
There are fleecy clouds[4] on the horizon,[4] and at sunset[3]
they take strange shapes[4] so that it is impossible not
20 to believe that you see a range of lofty mountains.[4]
They are the mountains[4] of the country of your dreams.[2]
You sail through an unimaginable[2] silence[4] upon a
magic sea.[1] Now and then a few gulls[4] suggest that
land[4] is not far off, a forgotten island[4] hidden in a wilder-
25 ness of waters;[1] but the gulls, the melancholy[2] gulls,[4]
are the only sign you have of it. You see never a tramp,[4]
with its friendly[2] smoke,[4] no stately bark[4] or trim
schooner,[4] not a fishing boat[4] even: it is an empty
desert,[1] and presently the emptiness[1] fills you with a
30 vague foreboding.[2]

soul of man." This triggers off a clear-cut *duality* in the text-structure, marked by adjectives (1.1 *inconstant*, 1.6 *arrogant*) which normally indicate human characteristics, but are used here to refer to the Pacific Ocean. A further important perspective is added by the *inclusion of the reader* in the text, who is repeatedly addressed as *you* (lines 8, 10, 11, 20, 21, 22, 26, 29), and is himself implicitly *characterized* as regards age (1.11 *vanished youth*), origin (one familiar with Beachy Head) and cultural background (1.13 the reference to Ulysses and a probable allusion to *The Merchant of Venice*, opening of Act V, Scene 1). Thus a second duality is created in a kind of *counterpoint technique*, whereby the Pacific is linked personally to the reader.

The adjectives *inconstant* and *uncertain* (1.1) motivate the series of *four impressionistic sketches* of the different moods of the Pacific, which determine the clear macro-structure of the text. The first sketch, introduced by the discourse marker *sometimes* (1.2), describes the ocean as *grey* and *rough*, the second, introduced by the marker *not so often* (1.5), as *calm* and *blue*. In the third sketch, introduced by *but* (1.14), the Pacific is *like a lake*, *flat and shining*, giving rise to a seascape description (1.15 *flying fish*, 1.18 *fleecy clouds*) which itself leads on to a final sketch introduced by *now and then* (1.23) characterizing the Pacific as barren, empty and lonely, the key-phrase being *wilderness of waters* (1. 24/5). There is a clear break in line 14 between the dynamic restlessness of the first two sketches and the static, unreal atmosphere of the rest of the text, as emerges from a succession of key-words like *heavy swell* (1.3), *boisterous* (1.5), *billows* (1.9), *desire for life* (1.12) on the one hand, and *strange shapes* (1.19), *unimaginable silence* (1.22) and *vague foreboding* (1.29) on the other. This type of lexical cohesion, which I have called *field progression*, will be discussed below.

First however, I should like to make a few brief comments on the syntax of this text. The sentences are characterized by *paratactic structure* with a striking number of *postmodifying phrases* (e.g. 1. 9/10: *The billows, magnificently rolling*), giving the text a syncopated, staccato rhythm. The verbs are insignificant, nearly all appear in the simple present tense, usually as monosyllables, frequently in an unstressed copula form of *to be*. This means that almost the entire message of the text is communicated by the nouns and adjectives and their varying modes of combination, these reflecting the duality of "Pacific" and "soul of man" which was pointed out above. Most of the *nouns* fall into one of two clear groups designating either the Pacific itself or elements of the seascape description connected with it: most of the

	Pacific	Man	Light	Seascape
1	Pacific	inconstant uncertain		
2		soul of man	grey	(English Channel)
3	heavy swell			(Beachy Head)
4	rough capped/crests		white	
5	calm	boisterous	blue	
6		arrogant	blue sun shines	
7		fiercely		unclouded sky trade wind
8		blood impatience		
9	billows			
10	rolling			
11		vanished youth memories		
12		restless, intolerable desire for life		
13	such a sea as this			
14	Pacific			Happy Isles
15	lake sea		shining	flying fish
16			gleam of shadow brightness	
17			sparkling	little fountains drops dip
18			sunset	fleecy clouds horizon
19				strange shapes
20				range of lofty mountains
21		dreams		mountains
22		unimaginable		silence
23	magic sea			few gulls
24	wilderness of waters	forgotten		land island
25		melancholy		gulls gulls
26				tramp
27		friendly stately trim		smoke bark schooner
28	empty desert			fishing boat
29	emptiness	foreboding		

adjectives on the other hand characterize the "soul of man," and there is a fourth group combining nouns and adjectives that indicate colour and light. Many of the adjectives (especially in the first half of the text down to line 15) are used predicatively and are hence in a stressed, focal position in the sentence. The description of the seascape in the second half, on the other hand, is characterized by noun phrases combining non-human seascape elements (*gulls, smoke, schooner*) and attributive adjectives indicating human characteristics (*melancholy, friendly, trim*).

On the basis of these observations we can trace a *progression of lexical fields* within the text.[5] The four columns on the diagram represent the lexical fields mentioned above as forming the lexical framework of the text: 1. those items specifically designating the Pacific, 2. those characterizing Man, 3. those indicating light (and colour), and 4. those indicating images or elements of the general seascape description. They are arranged vertically according to the lines of the printed text (indicated on the left). In the text itself (p. 71 above), Field 1 is indicated by *double* underlining, Field 2 by *single* underlining, Field 3 by *dotted* underlining and Field 4 by *wavy* underlining.

The progression of the fields within the text and in relation to each other emerges clearly from the diagram. The first part of the text (down to line 7) focusses on the duality Man/Pacific, the former expressed by *dynamic adjectives* (cf. 3.5 below) indicating behaviour (*boisterous, arrogant, fierce*), the latter by colour adjectives and terms referring to movement (*heavy swell, rough*) or the lack of it (*calm*). Then a connection is made to the reader (1.7, "The trade wind gets into your blood"), who is immediately put in central position (1.11, "you forget your vanished youth, with its memories, cruel and sweet, in a restless, intolerable desire for life"). With the reference to Ulysses (1.13) and the Happy Isles (1.14), a distant perspective ensues, as regards both time and place. The second half of the text focusses on the seascape, both in close-range detail (*flying fish*) and from a distance (*fleecy clouds on the horizon*), whereby the visual element gains prominence by the use of items indicating light (*gleam, brightness, sparkling*). The transition to the unreal emerges from the sequence (lines 18-23) *fleecy clouds — strange shapes — lofty mountains — country of your dreams — magic sea*. The introduction of *you* (1.20) reinstates the relationship between description and reader, which is maintained to the end of the text. The final part depicts an unreal world where the only elements actually present are the gulls, the other concrete items all being negated (*smoke, schooner, fishing boat*) or illusory (*forgotten island*). Highly prominent are the two related metaphors *wilderness of waters* and *empty desert*, the latter leading into the key-word *emptiness* (1.29) with the ominous feeling of foreboding it produces.[6]

The next stage of a macro-to-micro-level analysis would be an investigation of the key lexical items (here *inconstant, billows, gleam of shadow, wilderness, foreboding*). Lexical analysis is the subject of 3.5.1 below and reference to these items will be made there. For the present, we shall turn to the authorized German translation of "The Pacific" and see how it compares with the original in the light of what we have concluded so far.

The translation (reproduced on the following page) was published in 1953, before the rise of text-linguistics and before the emergence of translation studies as a subject of academic status, and indeed it shows some characteristic features of the time and of most translations where the text is viewed as a string of words and structures to be converted into a string of equivalents. We would not describe the text as a "bad translation": in itself, it forms a coherent and cohesive whole, without the startling howlers evident in some translations, and its weaknesses cannot be explained in terms of lexical items or linguistic incompetence. Grounds for criticism can however be detected if the text is viewed as a macro-structure and compared with the macro-structure of the original.

The English text and its authorized translation were discussed in three seminars with German-speaking students,[7] and all three groups came to similar conclusions, these relating directly to observations made in this section. The most frequent criticism made of the German translation was that it "lacked contour," was "flatter than the English text." The reason for this is connected with the twofold duality in the English original described above. Firstly, the reader is in no way involved in the German text, the *you*-form being rendered impersonally throughout,[8] resulting in stilted phrases like "die Wogen umgeben *einen* üppig" (1.10) and "... diese Leere *einen* erfüllt" (1.34). The one exception "Berge *unseres* Traumlandes" (1.25) is too weak to give the reader the vitality he has in the English text, all the more so as the omission of any phrase rendering "like the English Channel off Beachy Head" leaves the reader unidentified as regards origin, and the rendering of "your *vanished* youth" as "die *schwindende* Jugend" (1.11) blurs the characterization as regards age. Secondly, all three groups

Der Stille Ozean
(1953)

Der Stille Ozean[1] ist unbeständig[2] und wandelbar[2] wie
die Seele des Menschen.[2]/Manchmal liegt er grau[3] danmit
mächtiger Dünung,[1] manchmal ist er wild gebauscht[1] und
trägt weiße[3] Wellenkämme.[1]/Nicht häufig zeigt er sich
5   blau[3] und glatt,[1] dann aber ist er von anmaßendem[2] Blau.[3]
Hemmungslos brennt die Sonne[3] aus wolkenlosem Him-[4]
mel[4] hernieder. Der Passatwind[4] geht einem ins Blut[2] und
erfüllt es mit der ungeduldigen Forderung[2] nach dem
Unbekannten. Die hochaufrollenden Wogen[1] umgeben
10   einen üppig von allen Seiten, und man vergißt die
schwindende Jugend[2] mit ihren grausamen und süßen
Erinnerungen[2] vor lauter Sehnsucht,[2] dieser rastlosen,[2]
unaushaltbaren Sehnsucht nach Leben.[2]/Auf solch einem[1]
Meer[1] segelte Odysseus, als er die Glücklichen Inseln[4]
15   suchte./Doch gibt es auch Tage, da der Stille Ozean[1] sich
hinbreiten wie ein See.[1] Flach dehnt sich das Meer[1] aus
und glänzt.[3] Die fliegenden Fische,[4] eine Schattenhusch[3]auf
dem leuchtenden[3] Spiegel, lassen eine kleine Fontäne[4]
funkelnder[3] Tropfen aufperlen,[4] wenn sie wieder ins
20   Wasser tauchen.[4] Flockige Wolken[4] erscheinen am Hori-[4]
zont[4] und nehmen bei Sonnenuntergang[3] so seltsame[4]
Formen[4] an, daß man glaubt, ein hoher Gebirgszug türme[4]
sich auf.[4] Es sind Berge[4] unseres Traum[2]landes. So gleitet
man wie auf einem Zaubermeer[1] durch die unvorstell-[2]
25   bare[2] Stille.[4]/Hin und wieder lassen ein paar Möwen[4] die
Hoffnung[2] aufkommen, daß Land[4] in der Nähe ist, ein
vergessenes[2] Eiland,[4] inmitten dieser Wasserwüste.[1] Doch
die Möwen,[4] die melancholischen[2] Möwen,[4] sind das ein-
zige, was man zu sehen bekommt. Niemals begegnet
30   man einem Dampfer[4] mit seinem freundlichen[2] Rauch,[4]
niemals einem stattlichen[2] Barkschiff[4] oder einem schmuk-[2]
ken[2] Schoner,[4] nicht einmal einem Fischerboot;[4] man ist
wirklich in der Wüste.[1] Und da fängt es an, daß diese
Leere[1] einen erfüllt mit nebelhafter Ahnung.[2]

Berechtigte Übertragung von Ilse Krämer

confirmed that the clear duality of Pacific and Man is weakened and blurred in the German text; the explanation lies in the choice of key nouns and adjectives, hence in the area of lexical cohesion. A brief comparison of the English with the German field progression (reproduced on the following page) shows that the dynamic adjectives introducing the German text are weaker and less evocative of human behaviour than those in the English: Hence the key introductory adjective *inconstant* (meaning "fickle") is blurred into *unbeständig*, conventionally used to describe weather. *Arrogant* and *fiercely* are weakened into *anmaßend* and *hemmungslos*, the duality *rough/boisterous* is turned into *wild gebauscht* (1.3) which evokes neither man nor water. An examination of the key lexical items in both texts shows that in the German text these are changed or weakened in their function in the text as a whole (most significant is the reduction of the heavily loaded final word *foreboding* to *Ahnung*), and the translator was apparently looking for individual equivalents rather than recreating a progression within a structured whole, itself embedded in a cultural background. This leads us on to the question of perspective in the German translation: what is missing is the *point of reference* for the German reader provided in the English text by the comparison with the English Channel; this has a clear function in the text and could well be recreated in a comparison with the geographically similar North Sea. There remains the relationship between title and text: the title "Der *Stille* Ozean" makes explicit what is only suggested in the geographical name and Latin Hard Word *Pacific*; thus when "der stille Ozean" is described as "wild gebauscht" with "hochaufrollenden Wogen," an element of incongruity is introduced which is entirely foreign to the message of the original.

With an analysis of this kind translation problems are not solved, but the translator is made aware of them, and in the actual translation process he/she can then decide on which priorities are to shape the target text. Much of course depends, as was pointed out already (2.2) on the function the translation is to fulfil in the target culture. Clearly, the literary text differs from the instructions for use and the technical report (cf. 4 below), and this is all the more reason why literary translation should develop methods of analysis and investigation both to determine the envisaged role for the translated text in the target culture and to anticipate its possible reception by readers and critics.[9]

	Der Stille Ocean	Mensch	Licht	Seelandschaft
1	Der Stille Ozean	unbeständig wandelbar		
2		Seele des Menschen	grau	
3	mächtiger Dünung wild gebauscht			
4	Wellenkämme		weiße	
5	glatt		blau	
6		anmaßendem Hemmungslos	Blau Sonne	aus wolkenlosem Himmel
7		Blut		Passatwind
8		ungeduldigen		
9	hochaufrollenden Wogen	Forderung		
10				
11		schwindende Jugend		
12		Erinnerungen/Sehnsucht/dieser rastlosen,		
13	Auf solch einem Meer	unaushaltbaren Sehnsucht nach Leben		
14				die Glücklichen Inseln
15	der Stille Ozean			
16	See Meer			
17			glänzt Schattenhusch	fliegenden Fische
18			leuchtenden	kleine Fontäne
19			funkelnder	Tropfen aufperlen
20				ins Wasser tauchen flockige Wolken Horizont
21			Sonnenunter-gang	seltsame Formen
22				hoher Gebirgszug türme sich auf
23		Traum		Berge
24	Zaubermeer	unvorstellbare		
25				Stille ein paar Möwen
26		Hoffnung		Land
27	Wasserwüste	vergessenes		Eiland
28				Möwen
29		melancholischen		Möwen
30				Dampfer
31		freundlichen stattlichen		Rauch Barkschiff
32		schmucken		Schoner Fischerboot
33	Wüste			
34	Leere	Ahnung		

3.3 Scenes-and-frames semantics[10]

Text analysis and text production: both are essential to the translation process. In the preceding section we focussed on analysis, and this is what the vast majority of studies on translation have limited themselves to: the creative process of text (re-)production is still a neglected field in translation theory. A promising starting point for studies in this area might be the so-called "scenes-and-frames" semantics of Charles Fillmore, which is presented here and discussed in its relevance for the translation process.

In his conception of "scenes-and-frames" semantics (Fillmore 1977), Fillmore developed his own theory of meaning, pleading for "an integrated view of language structure, language behavior, language comprehension, language change and language acquisition" (1977:55), which marked a bold departure from the dogmas of American linguistics still dominant at the time. Clearly, his "integrated view" harmonizes with the one adopted here, as does his rejection of the "checklist theory" (cf. 1.3.1 above) in favour of prototype semantics. In Fillmore's view, prototypes are essentially experiential (compare the discussion of Rosch, 1.3.1 above):

> On this view, the process of using a word in a novel situation involves comparing current experiences with past experiences and judging whether they are similar enough to call for the same linguistic coding. (1977:57)

This linguistic coding constitutes the *frame*, a term Fillmore took from his own work in case grammar (*case frame*), whereby the verbal action is seen from a certain perspective prescribed by the verb.[11] In connection with scenes-and-frames semantics he uses the term *frame* (rather misleadingly):

> ... for referring to any system of linguistic choice — the easiest being collections of words, but also including choices of grammatical rules or grammatical categories — that can get associated with prototypical instances of scenes. (1977:63)

The term *scene* is here understood as follows:

> I intend to use the word *scene* — a word I am not completely happy with — in a maximally general sense, to include not only visual scenes but familiar kinds of interpersonal transactions, standard scenarios, familiar layouts, institutional structures, enactive experiences, body image; and in general, any kind of coherent segment, large or small, of human beliefs, actions, experiences, or imaginings. (1977:63)

In other words, the *scene* is the experienced or otherwise meaningful situation that finds expression in linguistic form. Scenes and frames constantly activate each other (frame-scene, scene-frame, scene-scene, frame-frame), whereby the degree of complexity can vary. In other words, a particular linguistic form, such as a phrase found in a text, evokes associations which themselves activate other linguistic forms and evoke further associations, whereby every linguistic expression in a text is conditioned by another one.

According to Fillmore, the scenes-and-frames approach offers distinct advantages for text analysis (as against the strictly linguistic methods of analyzing theme-rheme progression or cohesion), because it emphasizes the dynamic aspect of text-assimilation:

> Successful text analysis has got to provide an understanding on the part of the interpreter of an image or scene or picture of the world that gets created and filled out between the beginning and the end of the text-interpretation experience. (1977:61)

In this way, the linguistic form is related to the experience and the response of the reader — a familiar approach in literary studies, but then an innovation for linguistics and hence a bridge between the two disciplines. Fillmore's concept of text-assimilation likewise reminds one of approaches to *Rezeptionsästhetik* (theory of aesthetic response, cf. discussion of Iser 1976 under 4.1 below), trends in hermeneutics and recent developments in translation theory: first, the image of particular situation is evoked before the mental eye of the reader, and during the course of the text this situation becomes embedded in other situations to form a meaningful whole, that is, the background and motivation are clarified and the necessary connections, such as cause and effect, are made. Text-assimilation thus involves creating an inner world, and this depends considerably on the subjective experience on the reader; this explains why the same text can be interpreted in different ways.

The coherence of the text, in Fillmore's view, results from the interrelations created between the individual scenes to form a complex "scene behind the text"; this applies to both written texts and oral communication:

> The process of communication involves the activation, within speakers and across speakers, of linguistic frames and cognitive scenes. Communicators operate on these scenes and frames by means of various kinds of procedures, cognitive acts such as filling in the blanks in schematic scenes, comparing presented real-world scenes with prototypical scenes, and so on. (1977:66)

The connection between Fillmore's scenes-and-frames semantics and translation is not difficult to make. Firstly, the processes he describes can be identified with those already discussed in this study as being essential to translation: the process of understanding, of relating to situation and sociocultural background and to one's own experience. This differs substantially from the linguistically oriented translation theories based on equivalence, which in Fillmore's terminology would be a mere frame-frame activation. The translation process as interpreted in terms of the scenes-and-frames theory may be described as follows:

Translation is a complex act of communication in which the SL-author, the reader as translator and translator as TL-author and the TL-reader interact. The translator starts from a presented frame (the text and its linguistic components); this was produced by an author who drew from his own repertoire of partly prototypical scenes. Based on the frame of the text, the translator-reader builds up his own scenes depending on his own level of experience and his internalized knowledge of the material concerned. As a non-native speaker, the translator might well activate scenes that diverge from the author's intentions or deviate from those activated by a native speaker of the source language (a frequent cause of translation error).

Based on the scenes he has activated, the translator must now find suitable TL-frames; this involves a constant process of decision-making, whereby he depends entirely on his proficiency in the target language. It is at this stage of the translation process, where the translator shapes the new text, that has up to now been neglected in translation theory. The scenes-and-frames approach, which does not merely work with words and structures, but with a more holistic principle of interrelated textual elements, experience, perception and background situation, could provide a promising starting point.

This will now be illustrated on the basis of a comparatively simple German text and its translation into English:

Noch zwei Babys in Mexiko aus Krankenhaustrümmern gerettet

Bonn (AP)

Auf dramatische Weise sind in Mexico-Stadt noch einmal zwei Babys aus den Trümmern des Hauptkrankenhauses lebend geborgen worden.
5   Ein Streifenwagen holte drei Suchhunde mit ihren deutschen Hundeführern mit heulenden Sirenen vom Flugplatz zurück, wo sie schon mit den übrigen Mitgliedern der deutschen Rettungsmannschaft zum Rückflug in die Bundesrepublik
10   bereitstanden, nachdem in den Trümmern des Krankenhauses noch einmal Lebenszeichen gehört worden waren. Die Suchhunde konnten in kürzester Zeit die Stelle orten und die erfolgreiche Bergung der Babys einleiten. Die Lufthansa-
15   Maschine wartete solange, bis die drei Hunde mit ihren Führern wieder zurück waren. Insgesamt 51 Mitglieder deutscher Bergungstrupps kehrten mit dem Flugzeug am Mittwoch in die Bundesrepublik zurück.

The reader of the *Süddeutsche Zeitung* on Thursday, 3 October 1985 is confronted with three frames in the headline, these providing the basic information of the small article that follows:

- Noch zwei Babys ... gerettet
- in Mexiko
- aus Krankenhausstrümmern.

These are intended to activate the following scenes (in other words, knowledge of the following is presupposed):

- there was a disastrous earthquake in Mexico
- babies have already been found alive in the hospital ruins.

The scenes activated by the German reader are prototypical; that means that he can imagine the situation on the basis of what he knows from television, books and newspaper reports, and these images are idealized and simplified. He is unlikely to have personal experience of earthquakes, still less will he be able to reproduce an exact picture of the specific earthquake, the "real-life scene" in question.

A text analysis from the macro to micro level (see 3.2 above) shows three groups of linguistic frames: (1) lexical structure, (2) time sequence shown in verbs, and (3) deixis by means of adverbial particles. The lexical structure of this text is represented in the diagram on page 84.

These lexical frames activate the following scenes:

- scene of action: Mexico
  "change of scene": A. hospital   B. streets   C. airport
- *Scene 1:*   hospital ruins, rescue operation
- *Scene 2:*   police car with dogs and 3 members of rescue team
- *Scene 3:*   airport with rescue team
- *Scene 4:*   return to hospital scene (motivated by frame *Lebenszeichen*)
- *Scene 5:*   return to airport scene (motivated by *Rückflug*).

The sequence of events is made equally clear by the verb-forms, particularly tenses, while further deictic elements of time and space are realized by adverbial particles. The interplay of deixis and action can be reproduced as follows:

4. (l.1-3)   sind ... geborgen worden
2. (l.4)   holte (zurück)
1. (l.9)   (schon) bereitstanden
1. (l.9-11)   (nachdem) gehört worden waren
3. (l.11-12) konnten ... orten und ... einleiten
2-4 (l.14)   wartete solange
5. (l.15)   (bis) wider zurück waren
6. (l.16-17) kehrten ... zurück.

In other words, the chronological order of the events (as indicated by the numbers on the left) was as follows: signs were heard — rescue team about to fly home — police car came with dogs — dogs located babies — babies rescued — plane waited — dogs back at airport — rescue team flew home. This means that the grammatical frames are not characterized by linear progression, but also by "changes of scene."

We can now turn to the creative process of constructing the target-language text, as observed by the translator (the author of this study). It must however be emphasized — all the more so as we favour an integrated approach to translation — that scenes and frames were not the only criterion applied in the translation — equally important are pragmatic considerations such as the conventions of newspaper headlines (block language) and the journalistic style used in articles of this kind.[12] (Cf. 4.2.1 below.)

For the sake of simplicity we will assume that a British quality press publication, with a similar readership as the *Süddeutsche Zeitung*, plans to reproduce the German news item in its Saturday edition (i.e. with no great

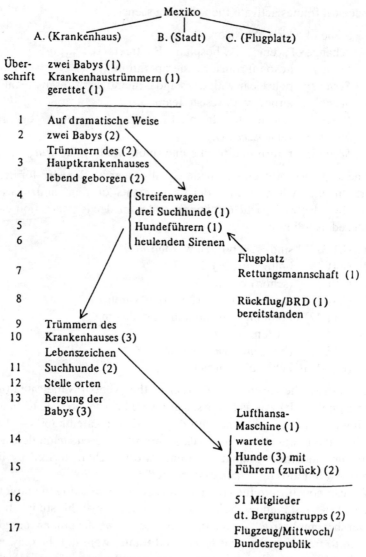

shift in time perspective), and has commissioned a German-English translation (i.e. with unchanged function, see 2.2 above).

The scenes activated by the translator as reader of the German article must be reconstructed into frames of the English language, again, not by matching word to word, but by the holistic process of recreating a gestalt. In English the following basic picture emerges:

Scene: *"Rescue"* — two more babies saved — dramatic rescue — sounds heard in hospital ruins — dogs located babies — rescue operation successful

Scene: *"Police car"* — rescue squad with specially trained dogs rushed to hospital site — police patrol car with sirens wailing

Scene: *"Airport"* — rescue workers already waiting at airport to return to Germany — plane waited until dogs were back — rescue team flew home.

From this we can now construct the following translation:

Two more babies saved from Mexico hospital ruins

It was a dramatic rescue for two babies found in the
ruins of Mexico City's Juarez Hospital last Wednesday.
Its sirens wailing, a police patrol car rushed to get
German rescue workers with three specially trained dogs
5 back from the airport — where they were already waiting
to fly back to Germany with the rest of the German rescue team — after sounds had been heard once again in the
hospital ruins. The dogs soon located the babies so that
the successful rescue operation could get under way. Mean-
10 while the Lufthansa plane waited until the three dogs
were back again with their masters. In all 51 members of
the German rescue squad flew home.

The sequence of events in the English text is determined by the following frame structure:

*4.	(l.1)	was ... found (last Wednesday)
2.	(l.3-5)	rushed to get ... back
*1-2	(l.5)	were (already) waiting
1.	(l.7)	(after) ... had been heard
*3a.	(l.8)	located
*3b.	(l.9)	could get under way
2-4.	(l.10)	(meanwhile) waited
5.	(l.11)	(until) ... were back again
6.	(l.12)	flew home.

This corresponds to the main structure of the German original, and the earliest event in the time sequence (*sounds ... had been heard*) is not mentioned until 1.7. There are however some slight shifts in time: the exact point in time (*last Wednesday*) results in change of tense and aspect (1.1); the progressive form *were ... waiting* (1.5) stresses durative verbal action running parallel to that effected by the police car. The act *located* (agent: *dogs*) and the process *get under way* (vehicle: *rescue operation*[13]) results in a succession of separate actions, as against parallel actions (*orten ... einleiten*) with identical agent (*Hunde*) in the German.

There are also slight shifts in perspective: the point of time is fixed as *last Wednesday*, referring to completed action effected a few days before publication of the text, and the spatial perspective is shifted by the transfer of the news item to England, where the reader has no personal or national relationship to the rescue team concerned. This also explains the wording of the last sentence: the point of time is here superfluous, and the phrase "kehrten mit dem Flugzeug ... in die Bundesrepublik zurück" becomes simply "flew home."

3.4 Speech acts and parallel texts

Whereas a translation is always derived from another text, parallel texts are two linguistically independent products arising from an identical (or very similar) situation. They are used in translation studies and lexicography (see Hartmann 1980 and 1989) for assessing how the same kind of factual material is verbalized in different languages. Stock examples are cooking recipes, instructions for use and public signs. In translator training, parallel texts are frequently used as aids in creating a natural and idiomatic translation (cf. 4.2 below).

The difference in reader response to poor translations on the one hand and idiomatic parallel texts on the other is effectively described by Vinay and Darbelnet in their *Stylistique comparée du français et de l'anglais* (1958) on the basis of public road signs: they express irritation at French-Canadian road signs (translated versions of the English signs familiar in the USA), which differ basically from authentic road signs in France (1958: 20). In such cases, parallel texts often represent the "model translation."

This section will be concerned with some authentic public directives in English and German: the aim is to investigate the complex relationship between communicative *function* and natural language *forms*, thus deriving some insights for translation theory. The theoretical basis, as is only suitable with directives of this kind, is the speech act theory as presented by Austin (1962) and developed by Searle (1969).

In order to distinguish clearly between form and function, we must make use of discrete terminology. In this section, which — after the textual focus in 3.2 and 3.3 — is essentially grammatical in approach, the term *sentence* will refer strictly to the unit of grammar, as realized in *declarative*, *interrogative* or *imperative* form. The term *utterance*, on the other hand, refers to the *functional* unit as element of communication and as realized in *statements*, *questions* and *directives* (for a more detailed explanation, see Snell-Hornby 1984b).

It is commonly believed that a declarative sentence is automatically a statement, that an interrogative sentence is invariably a question, and that an imperative sentence must essentially be a directive. In fact, the relation between grammatical form and communicative function is far more complex, and for the translator this is a vital insight. A so-called rhetorical question, for example, is in fact an *interrogative sentence* with the force of an emphatic *statement*, while a leading question combines the function of a statement and a question, the focus shifting according to specific factors. Thus form and function exist in a *dynamic tension* with each other,[14] and what is important for translation is the fact that this tension varies from one culture, and hence language, to another.

In Searle's terminology, the directive can be described as an illocutionary speech act with perlocutionary function. In other words, it expresses an *intention* on the part of the speaker to effect *future action* on the part of the addressee (cf. Snell-Hornby 1984c:207). The public directive is a text-type restricted to written language, as found in signs and notices displayed for public attention ("No smoking," "Cross now" etc.). The following analysis is based on empirical study of a corpus of 200 authentic public signs collected from various English- and German-speaking countries (USA, UK, India, Australia, FRG, Switzerland and Austria).

A detailed analysis of the corpus (selected examples are listed on the following page) and an explanation of the model used in the analysis can be found in Snell-Hornby 1984c. Here we shall present a summary of these findings and show their relevance for an integrated approach to translation studies.

The model presented here is similar in conception to the one representing the scope of translation studies under 1.4 above, in that it is a stratificational model with prototypical structures and concepts situated at points on a cline; in this case the cline ranges from request to prohibition. Once again the analysis proceeds from the macro-level of speech act type

Request (R)

1. Visitors are requested to stand at the beginning of each sitting when prayers are being offered by the President.
2. Passengers are kindly requested not to travel on the roof.
3. Will customers please note that all vehicles must be removed from the grounds by 5 p.m.
4. Please tender exact fare if possible.
5. Please don't let door slam.

6. Kunden werden höflichst gebeten, auf ihre Garderobe zu achten, da keine Haftung übernommen werden kann.
7. Um Wartezeiten zu vermeiden, bitten wir Sie, größere Abhebungen rechtzeitig anzukündigen.

Command (C)

1. Pedestrians use stairs.
2. Keep left.
3. Children under 12 years *must* be held at all times.
4. Slow — men at work. ———→

5. Wanderer! Erhalte den lebendigen Schmuck der Heimat! Verzichte auf das Pflücken von Blumen und Pflanzen!
6. Ruf doch mal an!
7. Schützt dieses Telefon! Es kann Leben retten.
8. Bitte halten Sie den Raum zwischen Fahrer und Tür *unbedingt* frei.
9. Einfahrt freihalten!
10. Hunde sind an der Leine zu führen.

Warning (W)

1. Beware of the bull!
2. Mind your head when leaving your seat.
3. Passengers entering or leaving the bus while it is in motion do so at their own risk.
4. Danger — keep out. ———
5. Trespassing vehicles will be towed away at the owner's risk and expense.
6. Emergency exit only! Alarm will sound.
7. Slippery when wet.

8. Warnung vor Dieben!
9. Achtung! Wagen schert aus.
10. Vorsicht bei laufenden Motoren. Vergiftungsgefahr.
11. Privatgrundstück. Benutzung auf eigene Gefahr.
12. Widerrechtlich abgestellte Fahrzeuge werden kostenpflichtig entfernt. ———→
13. Rauchmelder in Betrieb.

Prohibition (P)

1. No person shall bring into or consume intoxicating liquor in this park.
2. No dog will be allowed inside a Railway passenger compartment.
3. Children must not ride on the elevator unless they are accompanied by an adult.
4. Hawkers, canvassers, collectors not allowed.
5. Smoking strictly prohibited.
6. No passing.
7. Do not feed.
8. No food in this store!

9. Die Mitnahme von Tieren in die Mensa ist nicht gestattet.
10. Betreten der Eisfläche verboten.
11. Das Spielen der Kinder auf Hof, Flur und Treppe ist im Interesse aller Mieter untersagt.
12. Hausieren verboten.
13. Nicht füttern!

Cline ⟶
Hierarchy of levels ↓

Illocutionary Act (S Intention) ⟶ aim ⟶ Perlocutionary Effect (Ad Action)

	Request	Command	Warning	Prohibition
A. Speech Act Type	+/− Action	+/(−) Action	− Action	− Action
B. Participant Status	S ⤸ Ad	$\dfrac{S}{Ad}$	S ╲ Ad	$\dfrac{S}{Ad}$
Ad Identification	E/G + Ident	E +/(−) Ident · G +/− Ident	E +/− Ident · G − Ident	E +/− Ident · G − Ident
C. Grammatical Structure (Verb-form)	1. Imp. + adjunct 2. Main cl. vb. dep. cl. (reason) 3.	←IMPERATIVE E— 1. unmarked 2. modal vb. 3. verbless G— 1. marked 2. infin. 3. sind ... zu	hypothetical action / information 1. Future (passive) 2. Block language 3. Imp. (E only)	IMPERATIVE → neg. E— 1. unmarked 2. no + verbal noun 3. 4. verbless G— 1. infin. 2. past part. + verbal noun
D. Lexis	1. request, bitten 2. adjunct, particle	1. adverbial intensifier (unbedingt, at all times)	1. mind, beware 2. explicit abstract nouns 3. implicit specific lexemes	E— 1. not allowed, prohibited 2. adverbial intensifier (strictly, strengstens) G— verboten, nicht gestattet, untersagt

Stratificational model

S = speaker, Ad = addressee; E = English, G = German; Ident = identification/personalization down to the micro-level of lexis.

In both English and German the speech act types are identical, and there is no difference between the two languages as regards the relation between the two participants in the speech act, speaker and addressee: thus in either an English or a German request the speaker uses expressions of deference and courtesy to elevate the addressee to a level somewhat higher than himself, while in command and prohibition his situational position is clearly superior; in warnings the speaker is superior in that he possesses information and envisages consequences of which he assumes the addressee to be unaware (cf. B, Participant Status on the model reproduced above). It is at this point that the two languages begin to diverge (shown by the dotted line on the model). German and English differ essentially in the type of *identification* of the addressee in his situational role, and in his *personalization* by means of pronouns (subsumed under Ident. on the model). This applies particularly to warning and prohibition, where English favours imperatives (*beware*, *mind*) and identification, and German favours abstract nouns (*Warnung*, *Achtung*) without identification, as clearly emerges in these examples:

(3)	*Passengers* entering or			(11)	Privatgrundstück.
	leaving the bus while				Benutzung auf
	it is in motion do so				eigene Gefahr.
	at their own risk.

The focus on the identification of the addressee in English is also evident in the prominence of agentive nouns, as against verbal substantives in German, focussing on the action. This can be seen clearly in the two examples:

(4)	*Hawkers, canvassers,*			(12)	*Hausieren* verboten.
	collectors not allowed.

A further striking difference between the two languages is the absence of modal verbs in German as against English, illustrated by examples from the prohibition column:

(1)	No person *shall* bring into or consume ...
(3)	Children *must* not ride ...

but the main difference lies in the varying forms and usage of the imperative in German. English has only one form of the active, 2nd person imperative, and this is at the same time the basic *unmarked* form of the verb. Hence there is no formal change between "Keep still," as spoken to a child, and "Keep left," as on a road sign. Because of this formal and functional identity, the addressee of the public notice is appealed to in basically the same way as the specific hearer of the spoken command. The one, unmarked English form corresponds functionally to four forms in German, three of which are *marked* according to the form of address *du*, *ihr* or *Sie*, as in these examples in the Command column:

(6)   *Ruf* doch mal an![15]

(7)   *Schützt* dieses Telefon! Es kann Leben retten.[15]

(8)   Bitte *halten Sie* den Raum zwischen Fahrer und Tür unbedingt frei.

(emphasis added)

These all aim at appealing to the addressee personally, but on a different basis: the *du*-imperative has a psychological, individual appeal — here in (6) to rouse a wish; the *ihr*-imperative (7) appeals to him as one of many, rouses his sense of public spirit, and the *Sie*-imperative (8) addresses him as a responsible, adult member of society. Against that the impersonal infinitive form as in:

(9)   Einfahrt freihalten!

is open and unmarked, it leaves the addressee unpersonalized — and it is this form that is used with imperative function in most German public directives, as against the more personal unmarked imperative form in the English verb.

On the lexical level German prohibitions are characterized by the past participle form *verboten* (or its more formal stylistic variants *untersagt* and *nicht gestattet*), a fact which has led even serious-minded scholars to infer a German-speaking "Verbotsmentalität" (cf. Güttinger 1963:16 and comments in Snell-Hornby 1984c). The simple solution is that against the one lexeme in German there are several variants in English, and (as a glance at the list from the corpus will confirm) a wide variety of grammatical structures (apart from the modal verbs, the determiner *no* is commonly used, as in (6) and (8) of the prohibitions). The English lexical variants are not merely matters of style and formality, as in German. The lexeme *forbid* with past participle *forbidden* typically denotes a private act of a personal instigating agent (such as an authoritarian parent), and a typical utterance uses *forbid* as a performative verb as in "I forbid you to do that again!" It is for these reasons that *forbid* is hardly ever found in public directives. In a public context, with an impersonal public authority as agent (and usually in reference to some law or written regulation), the Hard Word *prohibit* is used (as in (5) of our English prohibitions), which thus has a different legal status and hence pragmatic function from *forbid*.[16] More neutral is the passive formation *not allowed*, less personal than *forbid*, less public than *prohibit*, the typical authorizing agent being an institution such as a boarding school.

The conclusion that emerges from the above is that German and English use different strategies, different grammatical structures and different lexical variants in what is fundamentally a similar situation. Seen from another perspective, we find a similar dynamic tension between grammatical form and communicative function in German as was established for English, but again with subtle differences in realization. If we take the command as the realization of the affirmative imperative and the prohibition as the realization of the negative imperative, the following picture emerges: in the case of commands both languages favour some form of the imperative, but they differentiate with diverging means: German with the various forms of the imperative as discussed above, English by identification of the addressee and by varying constructions with the adjunct *please* (see (3), (4) and (5) under Request). English favours modal verbs more than German (the structure occurring in (10) normally being the only one found in German commands[17]). The English example (4) is block language, typical of road signs, with an ellipted imperative construction "(Drive) Slow(ly)" and an explanatory (likewise elliptical) statement "Men (are) at work." The prohibitions present a different picture however: the negative imperative is only used in one example of each language, (7) and (13). In all other cases the prohibition is realized in the form of a *declarative* sentence, whether expressed in full grammatical form as (1), (2), (3), (9) and (11), or in block language as in (4), (5), (6), (8), (10) and (12).

The conclusion we can draw from this, that prohibition in public directives is typically realized, not in imperative, but in declarative form both in German and English, can be borne out by numerous other examples not included here. The obvious counter-example is "Keep off the grass," a directive which has however gradually been superseded by more subtle expressions. On the lawns of Exeter university campus, for example, is a notice, strategically placed to be legible from the paths, that reads: "Your feet are killing the Spring bulbs." This is of dubious truth-value as a statement; but as a directive this declarative sentence has proved to be singularly successful.

For translation theory the conclusions that can be drawn from this analysis are these: firstly, the main criterion for the translation of directives is the situation, the complex speech act itself with its entire constellation of participant relationships, communicative effect and linguistic variants; it cannot be the aim of the translation in such cases to "preserve the syntax of the original." And secondly the tension, often even discrepancy, between grammatical form and communicative function observed here is, as the experienced translator can confirm, a frequent phenomenon in language and hence a problem in translation.

A third important aspect is again the cultural background. Example (2) *k* in the Request column, "Passengers are kindly requested not to travel on the roof," may strike the European as being a little bizarre. This was a sign displayed in Hindi and English on the railway station of Old Delhi, hence in a society where rooftop-riding is quite common. As it is also a method of fare-dodging however and hardly a safe mode of travel, the courteous request construction is striking; the European expects a warning such as "Passengers travelling on the roof do so at their own risk" or "Roof-top riders will be prosecuted." Here too the answer can be found in the cultural background of India, particularly in the influence of Hindi, which favours request-forms in public directives. This is a common feature of speech-acts across the cultures. Another example from India, frequently cited by Vermeer (cf. Vermeer 1986) is the fact that Indian languages lack a word for "thank-you" because thanks are expressed by gesture. Indians "show thank-you" instead of saying it; what is in Europe a speech act is there "extralinguistic reality" — for translation studies a striking instance of translation as a cross-cultural event.

3.5 Dynamics in meaning

It was a legacy of structuralism that meaning was for some decades banned from linguistic studies.[18] Even when semantics was accepted as a respectable subject of linguistic research, it was treated as something quite separate from syntax — an attitude that has continued until quite recently. It is the aim of this chapter to show that syntax and semantics, grammar and meaning, structure and word are in fact interdependent, and that an integration of the two branches of language study are essential for the translator.

The concept of the dynamic adjective was at first strictly grammatical:

it goes back to a distinction first made in 1970 by Lakoff, then still a supporter of transformational grammar, in his study *Irregularity in Syntax*, and then developed by Quirk et al. in *A Grammar of Contemporary English* (1972). It is Quirk's conception of *dynamic* (in the grammar extended to verbs and nouns) that is of interest here: a *dynamic adjective* (cf. Quirk and Greenbaum 1973:124) can be used with the progressive aspect and the imperative as against a *stative adjective*, which cannot, hence:

(1)   John was being *careful* (dynamic)
       but not: *John was being tall (stative)

(2)   Be careful! (dynamic)
       but not: *Be tall!

We can therefore conclude from this that *careful* is a dynamic adjective, whereas *tall* is not. Exactly the same tests can be carried out on verbs: *eat, walk, stare, laugh* can be used in the progressive forms and are hence dynamic verbs, whereas *know* and *contain* do not admit the progressive or imperative and are hence categorized as stative (Quirk and Greenbaum 1973:21, 46f.).

Within the field of lexical semantics, Leisi used the same distinction, "static and dynamic properties", with reference to the adjective (Leisi 1975:42) in his book *Der Wortinhalt*, first published in 1953. No mention of him is made however by Lakoff, Quirk or other English-speaking grammarians, neither does Leisi refer to the English linguists in the later editions of his book, although the same distinction is being made — one from the lexicological, one from the grammatical angle — using similar examples.[19] It is a good example of the non-communication between languages and subdisciplines.

My own expanded definition of the dynamic adjective focusses on semantic criteria, although Quirk's grammatical observations also apply — not by chance but, as we shall see, as a logical consequence. While stative adjectives refer to such *inherent* properties as size, shape and substance (*tall, circular, liquid*), dynamic adjectives *characterize action or behaviour*, they refer to properties *either viewed as temporary or changeable* or else applied *externally as a value-judgement* or *experienced as sensuous perception* (*careless, cruel, dazzling, noisy*). In expressing a value-judgement or describing perceptions, dynamic adjectives are susceptible to subjective measure (cf. Quirk and Greenbaum 1973:125[20]), thus reflecting the individual attitude of the speaker. In being gradable, the dynamic adjective permits variations in degree and measurement on a scale; hence its value is relative and can be judged in terms of an implied *norm*, whether set personally by the speaker or imposed by the social environment and implicitly accepted by the speaker (*slow*, *vulgar*, *naughty*). It is important to realize however, that the dividing-line between the stative and the dynamic adjective is by no means as clear-cut as Quirk and Leisi seem to indicate in their categorization, and much depends on use in context: here again, we are dealing, not with binary opposites specifying two discrete categories into which all adjectives can be neatly divided, but with two prototypes, two outer areas of a continuum or cline, with a central grey area dependent on usage. As an abstract concept, *stative* refers essentially to inherent, stable, objectively measurable qualities, and *dynamic* refers to temporary qualities dependent on subjective perception or measure and external value-judgement. It is the temporary nature of what is denoted by the dynamic adjective that permits the combination with the progressive and imperative forms of the verb. The rule is not merely restricted to grammatical form: semantics and syntax here interact.

This abstract concept of dynamics in meaning is however by no means limited to the adjective, but — as emerges from Quirk's grammar — is recognizable in all the open classes of lexeme. It is the central aspect of what I have identified as verb-descriptivity (Snell-Hornby 1983), as illustrated by the verbs *bustle*, *gleam*, *grovel* or *waft*, and it is present in nouns like *hag*, *thug* or *hovel*. In language learning and translation, dynamic adjectives, descriptive verbs and nouns with dynamic evaluation are a notorious source of difficulty and error — and they are at the same time given unsatisfactory treatment in bilingual dictionaries. The reasons are actually obvious: sociocultural norms are elusive factors that both change with time and vary from one language community to another, while evaluation and perception complicate the lexical item by adding perspectives that go beyond the purely linguistic.

It is at this point that the problems of the bilingual dictionary as an aid to translation should be taken up in our discussion, because there seems to be an unbridgeable gap between the convictions of lexicologists (as theoretical linguists) and bilingual lexicographers on the one hand, and the actual needs of the translator as dictionary user, on the other.[21] Up to now theoretical work on bilingual lexicography has been based on the assumption that the dictionary article must necessarily offer foreign language equivalents which would replace the source-language headword in what is misleadingly called the "slot of the text" — whereby the text is yet again viewed as a mere chain of items and the translation a string of dictionary equivalents. Zgusta (1984:147) for example writes as follows:

> The dictionary should offer not explanatory paraphrases or definitions, but real lexical units of the target language which, when inserted into the context, produce a smooth translation. This is a perfectly natural requirement. Lexicographers have followed it since time immemorial.

Zgusta's last sentence is of course factually correct, and that is precisely the problem, both for translation and of lexicography. In similar vein, Kromann et al. (1984) list the advantages bilingual dictionaries are supposed to have over monolingual ones for the translator, such as, for example, that they offer "immediately insertable equivalents" (1984:108).

For the translator the main problem lies in the frequent discrepancy between lexemes viewed in isolation and their usage as words in context. Here again we are faced with the "dynamic tension" existing between system, norm and text (see 2.3 above). In this conception the dynamic adjective, as an abstract notion, is a product of the language system, while the dictionary entry represents the unmarked norm as language potential (cf. Hanks 1988 and Stolze 1988). For the translator it is a source of eternal fascination to see how this potential can be exploited creatively in the concrete text.

To illustrate this, I should like to take the text as starting-point; for this purpose three non-literary texts have been chosen. From the word in context we shall then proceed to the isolated lexeme in the dictionary.

The three texts under discussion, one German and two English, all describe various aspects of the north of England. The German article from *Die Zeit* (the present discussion will be limited to the introduction, reproduced on the following page) describes the industrial north as a prospective tourist centre of the 21st century. The text has been used both in linguistic seminars and in translation classes, where it proved to be a lexicological goldmine with abundant examples showing that translation cannot take place by simply inserting dictionary equivalents. One example is the title, recognizable as an adaptation from Karl Marx "Proletarier aller Länder, vereinigt euch!", the allusion being critical for its effect. The problem is one

DIE ☙ ZEIT   Information · Hintergrund: Seite 64   REISE

Nr. 13 - 23. März 1984   Seite 55

Venezianische -Schlote, korinthische Bahnhöfe, gotische Börsen –
die Altertümer der industriellen Revolution sind reif für den Tourismus

Reisende aller Länder, vereinigt Euch

Zwischen York und Liverpool döst das größte
Freilichtmuseum der Welt / Von Cordt Schnibben

Wie Kreuze auf den Vampir, so wirken Fabrikschornsteine auf den Touristen. Er macht kehrt. Großbritannien als Reiseland hat darum in der Mitte, da, wo die Insel von mächtiger Hand zusammengequetscht wurde, ein **5** touristisches Niemandsland, einen großen, schwarzen Fleck. Unten sitzt London, links liegt walisisches Grün, oben hängt schottische Wildnis – aber in der Mitte, da ist das düstere Nichts. Attention! No travelling area!   **10**

Ausgerechnet dieses Nichts ist das größte Freilichtmuseum der Welt. Kitschiger als Disneyland, atemberaubender als Serengeti, lehrreich wie der Louvre. . Vollgestopft mit urigen Bauten und klapprigen Maschinen, mit lieblichen Fabriken und schnuckeligen Arbeitervierteln. Die Werkstatt der Welt, die Wiege der Industrie, sie ist noch ziemlich gut erhalten.

Vor zweihundert Jahren begann hier, zwischen York und Liverpool, die industrielle Revolution. Sie krempelte England und die Welt um wie nichts davor und nichts danach. Sie schuf neue Maschinen wie am Fließband, setzte Fabriken und die Landschaft, ließ Dörfer im Geldrausch zu Großstädten anschwellen.

Schon hundert Jahre später war der Zauber allerdings vorbei. Amerika überflügelte die Insel und holte den Titel „Land der unbegrenzten Möglichkeiten" über den Teich. England ging unter, und immer mehr seiner Schornsteine gingen aus.

Ein paar Jahrhunderte nach dem Untergang von Wirtschaftsmetropolen pflegen wir Touristen uns am Ort des versunkenen Reichtums einzufinden. Den minoischen Palästen erging es so, den Banken Sienas und den Handelshäusern Venedigs. Den frühkapitalistischen Kathedralen und industriellen Tempeln wird es genauso ergehen – in einigen Jahrzehnten. Wer sie jetzt schon besucht, schlägt

A

dem Massentourismus ein Schnippchen. Die Reisenden des nächsten Jahrhunderts werden über York in die Industriepark strömen. Zum einen, weil die Stadt schon heute über das nötige touristische Know-how verfügt. Denn ihre Glanzzeit liegt noch weiter zurück, so daß der Fremdenverkehr bereits genügend Zeit hatte, sich auszubreiten. Zum anderen gibt sie ein schönes Bild vom England vor der industriellen Revolution.

Mittelalterliche Gassen mit schiefen Fachwerkhäusern, eine mächtige Stadtmauer und natürlich **50** das verzuckerte Münster lassen romantische Herzen schneller schlagen. Und wem der nackte Stein zu kalt ist, der kann im Burgmuseum, Englands populärstem Volkskundemuseum, präindustrielle Stadtluft schnuppern. Der kann in Schlafgemächer **55** lugen und schauen, in welchen Zimmern elegante Georgianer speisten, wohlhabende Gutsbesitzer sich wärmten und gewöhnliche Heidebauern hausten.

Das Mittelalter in York hat allerdings einen Schönheitsfehler. Einen ziemlich schönen Bahn- **60** hof. Nicht weit von der Kathedrale schwingen sich die feinen Bogenrippen der vier grazilen Hallenschiffe kühn über die Gleise. Gestützt auf schlanke Säulen, überspannen sie luftig-leicht siebzig Meter und reihen sich zu einem Palast von 250 Meter Länge. „Prächtiges Monument der Extravaganz", nörgelte seinerzeit ein ebenso giftiger wie geiziger Aktionär der Eisenbahngesellschaft. Auch heute noch stören die wenigen ein- und ausfahrenden Züge das Kunstwerk beträchtlich.

B

of dimension in language as discussed under 2.4 above, and again the translation must *recreate the dimensions* rather than present a string of equivalent lexemes (of the type "Travellers of all lands, join together"). The
desired effect is achieved by adapting the standard TL version of the Marx
directive, and the translation strategies can be generalized as follows:

(1)   From the *SL variant* the translator must *recognize* the *SL original*
       (or prototype)

(2)   He/she must know (or find out) the corresponding *TL prototype*.

(3)   He/she must adapt the TL prototype to *recreate* the *SL variant*.

With reference to this example, the steps are as follows:

(1)   SL variant (*Reisende* aller Länder) goes back to the original
       "*Proletarier* aller Länder...."

(2)   The TL prototype is "Workers of the world, unite!"[22]

(3)   The TL variant therefore runs: "Travellers of the world, unite!"

This is a simple example of a frequent phenomenon in translation, and the
translator usually has to rely entirely on his background knowledge. A dictionary of quotations and proverbs with the originals or prototypes in different languages might help, but the translator still has to distinguish variants and recognize originals. Nothing can free him from the first of the steps
listed above, without which no dictionary can provide an "immediately
insertable equivalent."[23]

A similar problem is found in the same text (A, 1.5-10), where the
writer alludes to the map of Britain, concentrating on the part "wo die Insel
von mächtiger Hand zusammengequetscht wurde," which he describes as
"ein touristisches *Niemandsland*, einen großen schwarzen Fleck." What is
important here is not so much the combined denotations of the two lexemes
schwarz + *Fleck* as they would appear in their separate dictionary definitions, but the effect produced by the play on the phrase *weißer Fleck*, meaning a still unexplored area on the map (the privative sense standing in
apposition to *Niemandsland* and echoed later in the word *Nichts*, lines 9
and 11), whereby *schwarz* evokes the grime, the all-pervasive soot of the
industrial North (this again being echoed by *düster* in l.9). What is meant is
therefore a privative, a "grimy blank" (from the tourist's point of view)

rather than a "black stain," as resulted in students' translations from the combination of dictionary equivalents. An evocative dynamic adjective frequently used in English to describe precisely this aspect of the industrial north is the lexeme *bleak*, as is found in the extract from TIME magazine (reproduced page 101), a text which complements the German one by describing the industrial town of Barnsley during the miners' strike in 1984. *Bleak* (A, 1.8) is a prototypical dynamic adjective, expressing essentially the speaker's subjective perception and evaluation. The entries in the *Advanced Learner's Dictionary* (ALD), the *Concise Oxford Dictionary* (COD) and the *Collins English Dictionary* (CED), reproduced below, show the difficulties provided by the dynamic adjective even for the monolingual dictionary:

ALD   **bleak** /blik/ *adj* **1** (of the weather) cold and cheerless; (of a place) bare, swept by cold winds: *a* ∿ *hillside.* **2** (fig) dreary: ∿ *prospects.* ∿**·ly** *adv*

COD   **bleak²**, a. Wanting colour; bare, exposed, windswept; chilly; dreary. [16th c., of obsc. phonology; rel. to obs. *bleach*, obs. *blake* (= OE *blāc*, ON *bleikr*) pale, ult. f. Gmc **blaik-*; see BLEACH]

CED   **bleak¹** (bli:k) *adj*. **1.** exposed and barren; desolate. **2.** cold and raw. **3.** offering little hope or excitement; dismal: *a bleak future.* [Old English *blāc* bright, pale; related to Old Norse *bleikr* white, Old High German *bleih* pale] —'**bleak·ly** *adv.* —'**bleak·ness** *n.*

In all cases the definitions are typically rendered by a string of quasi-synonyms, which are either too general (*cold*) or are other, equally opaque, dynamic adjectives (*dreary*). What is focal about the lexeme *bleak* is not objective coldness or verifiable lack of vegetation, but the speaker's *experience* of lacking warmth, colour and comfort. Hence the moorland landscape of Yorkshire — whose bleakness is so effectively communicated in Emily Bronte's *Wuthering Heights* — is in fact largely covered by heather and can be quite colourful.

The entries from the bilingual dictionaries *Wildhagen* (Wi), *Langenscheidts Enzyklopädisches Wörterbuch* (LEnz) and *Pons/Collins* (P/C) also provide lists of quasi-synonyms:

WI   **bleak** [bliːk] a (~ly adv) *kahl, öde* ‖ *unge-*
         schützt, zugig ‖ *rauh, kalt, frostig* ‖ ⟨fig⟩ *trübe,*
         traurig, freudlos ~**ness** ['~nis] s *Kälte, Rauheit* f
         ‖ (of a site) *Ungeschütztheit* f, *zugige Lage* f

LEnz   **bleak²** [bliːk] *adj* 1. kahl, öde, ohne
         Vegetati'on. – 2. ungeschützt, windig
         (gelegen). – 3. rauh, kalt, scharf
         (*Wind, Wetter*). – 4. *fig.* kalt, freudlos,
         traurig, trübe. – 5. *obs. od. dial.* bleich,
         blaß. — '**bleak·ness** *s* 1. Kahlheit *f*,
         Öde *f*. – 2. Rauheit *f*, Schärfe *f*. —
         '**bleak·y** *adj* etwas kahl *od.* öde.

P/C   **bleak** [bliːk] *adj* (+*er*) 1. öde, trostlos.
         2. *weather, wind* rauh, kalt. 3. (*fig*) trost-
         los; *existence also* freudlos.

Looking at the TIME description of Barnsley during the miners' strike, one wonders how the translator would be helped by either Wi or LEnz in his rendering of *bleak* (epitomized in the photograph of the town): none of the intended equivalents in these two dictionaries are "insertable," especially as the cohesion of the text requires a suitable antonym to "pride of York-shire." The most accurate synonym is the equally subjective epithet and dynamic adjective *trostlos* offered by P/C, but even here there is no indica-tion as to why this is so, and the translator has to rely on his general knowl-edge and intuition.

Another problem presented by *bleak*, as is typical of dynamic adjec-tives, is its figurative usage, illustrated (A, l.37): "One miner has prepared his children for a bleak holiday ahead by telling them Father Christmas is dead." This lexicalized metaphor, in the sense of "bleak prospects" (ALD), "bleak future" (CED), carries the meaning of German *freudlos* (as suggested by P/C with explicit reference to *existence*), but the translator would find little guidance, let alone an immediately insertable equivalent, in either of the other two dictionaries.

The section of the German text marked (B) on p. 97 above, describes the Castle Museum in York with information very similar to that in the offi-cial guide-book of York as reproduced page 103 (B, dotted underlining). We are here concentrating on the lexeme *hausen* (l.58). What is being referred to here is the moorland cottage kitchen reproduced in the photo-graph. *Hausen* is a verb meaning "to live under conditions felt by the speaker to be squalid or inadequate" (cf. Snell-Hornby 1983:107). Here too the dynamic aspect of evaluation and perception is dominant, as emerges

"We've Been Wounded"

"Are there any museums in Barnsley?" asked a skeptic on hearing that the Metropolitan Bureau Council had applied for a grant to stimulate the tourist trade. "Certainly," shot back a city father. "Sixteen coal pits! They are all museums!"

5   The gritty humor is typical of Barnsley (pop. 75.000). located at the foot of the rain-drenched Pennines 180 miles northwest of London. The city officials like to describe
A   Barnsley as the "pride of Yorkshire." "Bleak" and "black" are more like it, according to the *Blue Guide*, a leading
10 guide-book. Fully 20% of the area's male population are miners on strike; an additional 18% of the work force are without jobs. Says Barnsley Businessman Robin Gibson: "We've been wounded."

In Barnsley, coal is king and strike sentiment is high. The
15 city's soot-blackened, lace-curtained row houses are built over a network of exhausted mine shafts. On the outskirts of town stands an ornate memorial to the gener-
20 ations of men and boys who have "gone down the pits" and lost their lives. More than 16,000 miners live in the area. Before the miners'
25 dispute began, they were known as big spenders, spreading much of their wages—totaling $2.4 million a week—in and around
30 Barnsley's stores, shops and pubs. All that has changed. Now many of Barnsley's miners exist on handouts, soup kitchens and social se-
35 curity benefits. One miner has prepared his children for a bleak holiday ahead by
A   telling them Father Christmas is dead.

Terraced houses set near one of Barnsley's ailing factories

from the German definitions in the *Wörterbuch der deutschen Gegenwartssprache* (WdG), *Duden* (Du) and *Brockhaus-Wahrig* (BW):

WdG   hausen /*Vb.*/
1. (*unkultiviert*) *wohnen* a) *unter schlechten Bedingungen, dürftig leben*: in den zerstörten Städten mußten viele Menschen in Kellerwohnungen h.; die Flüchtlinge hausten in Baracken b) *abgesondert, sittenlos und ungezügelt leben*: auf dieser Burg haben früher die Raubritter gehaust; in den Wäldern hausten Räuber c) umg. scherzh. wo haust du jetzt eigentlich?; hier h. wir!; wie er dort haust, ist fabelhaft. Ein wahres Schloß am Meer ist sein Th. Mann 11,308

BW   'hau·sen (V. 410) 1 (411) *in ärmlichen Verhältnissen, unter menschenunwürdigen Bedingungen wohnen;* sie müssen in einer Baracke ~; er hauste ein Jahr in dem halb verfallenen Haus; zu zehnt auf einem Zimmer ~ 1.1 *abgesondert in Wäldern, Bergen usw. leben;* hier hausten vor vielen Jahren die Räuber 1.2 (umg.; scherzh.) *wohnen;* hier hause ich jetzt; du haust also vorübergehend bei Freunden?

Du   hausen ['hauzn] (sw. V.; hat.' [mhd. hūsen; ahd. hūson = wohnen, sich aufhalten; beherbergen; wirtschaften; später auch: übel wirtschaften; sich wüst aufführen): 1.a) (ugs. abwertend) *unter schlechten Wohnverhältnissen leben;* in einer Baracke, einer Hütte h.; Oder diese kleinen Zimmer, in denen wir zu viert h. mußten (Hörzu 29, 1972, 32); b) (abwertend) *abgesondert, einsam wohnen, so daß niemand Einblick in die Lebensweise bekommt;* auf abgelegenen Burgen hausten Raubritter; Warum geht sie nicht hin und mietet irgendwo eine Kammer, wo sie in Ruhe h. kann (Werfel, Himmel 151); c) (ugs. scherzh.) *wohnen;* wir hausen jetzt in einer gemütlichen, kleinen Dachwohnung; Du weißt, es gefällt ihnen gar nicht, daß ich hier bei dir hause (Baldwin [Übers.], Welt 314).

Here the dynamic adjectives *schlecht* (WdG, Du), *dürftig* (WdG), *ärmlich* (BW) and *menschenunwürdig* (BW) are focal.

Looking at the picture of the moorland cottage reproduced opposite (with ornaments on the mantelpiece and homemade rugs on the floor), one may wonder whether *hausen* is in fact an accurate description. The reader familiar with the museum itself may suspect that the German author has attempted a translation equivalent of the word "spartan" used by the museum authorities to describe the life of the moorland peasants in the printed information displayed outside the room with the cottage kitchen. Another explanation is that in the German text the function of *hausen* is clearly to underline the contrast with the rooms of the richer families (*Schlafgemächer, elegante Georgianer, wohlhabende Gutsbesitzer*). A more prototypical context to illustrate *hausen* is the following extract from the *Süddeutsche Zeitung* on overcrowded prisons in the USA (SZ, 12.4.1984):

Die neue Gesellschaft begann das Geschäft zunächst mit der Einwanderungsbehörde. Der Bau einer Haftanstalt für 300 illegale Einwanderer in Houston, Texas, ist nahezu beendet, das Projekt
5   wird fünf Millionen Dollar kosten, und die Einwanderungsbehörde zahlt 23,50 Dollar pro Tag und Insasse. Ein bescheideneres Projekt in Los Angeles ist bereits in Betrieb, hier hausen 125 Illegale hinter Stacheldraht, Männer, Frauen und
10   Kinder, für die ebenfalls der gleiche Pro-Kopf-Betrag kassiert wird. Es ist noch alles etwas primitiv und unbequem, doch für so wenig Geld könne niemand etwas Besseres bieten, meint die Firma.

CASTLE MUSEUM

THE VISION OF DR J L KIRK

At the beginning of this century, John Lamplugh Kirk was a young country doctor at Pickering, a market town about 25 miles from York. He realised before anyone else that many of the objects used for centuries in the everyday life of country people — farmers, craftsmen, shopkeepers and many others — were fast disappearing with the advent of mass production, and he began to collect them. He collected anything and everything that could be called a bygone, and which to most other people was just junk. Finally in 1935 he presented his outstanding collections to the City of York and spent the next three years converting the disused Female Prison into a museum.

Today the Castle Museum is one of the most successful folk museums in the world.

Half Moon Court

This is the Edwardian counterpart of Kirkgate with more shops and a granite drinking fountain. The star attraction is undoubtedly the King William IV Hotel, a fine pub, resplendent with gleaming brass rails and gas-burners and complete with a penny-in-the-slot musical box. The electrician displays his fantastic new inventions and the ironmonger sells everything from door-knobs and carpet-beaters to razors, soap and jam-pot covers. Hardings, the drapers, sells fine linen and sheets at 15s. 11d. per pair. The garage houses two early cars, the Grout of 1899 being powered by steam.

York – Official Guide

                                B

THE KIRK COLLECTION

The Period Rooms and Galleries

The stairway leads to the fascinating Period Room Gallery with a Victorian Parlour and Moorland Cottage, Georgian Dining Room and 17th century hall and coming right up to date, the Coronation Sitting-Room of 1953.

A moorland cottage kitchen

DEBTORS' PRISON

Downstairs is a fascinating costume exhibition including a Georgian bedroom scene, a wedding dress and a dazzling display of jewellery and fans. The costume is changed regularly to reflect the diversity of the collection. Period toys include a clockwork tiger, and the Edwardian bathroom echoes the elegance of the country house.

Here a privately run prison is being described where 125 illegal immigrants
are *crowded together* behind *barbed wire* with the additional comment that
it is "noch alles etwas primitiv und unbequem" (1.11/12). This example
comes closer to the unmarked dictionary norm than does the one describing
the moorland cottage kitchen. In any case however, *hausen* is an item
notoriously difficult to translate into English and inadequately treated in
bilingual dictionaries (cf. Holzheuser 1986). Three examples are given
here, from Wi, P/C and *Harrap's Concise* (HC):

Wi

> h·**ausen** vi [h] **1.** (wohnen) *to dwell,
> live (in caverns); reside;* wir ~ schon lange hier
> *we have resided here for a long time;* ~ **in** .. *to
> inhabit (a place);* in verfallenen Wohnungen ~
> *to live in tumble-down dwellings* | wie Schweine
> zus–~ *to herd together like pigs; to pig* (mit *with*);
> *to pig it*

P/C

> **ha̲u̲sen** *vi* **1.** (*wohnen*) to live.
> ...

HC

> h ~ **en** ['-zɔn], *v.i.*
> (*haben*) (*a*) to live, *F:* hang out (**bei** j-m, with
> s.o.); (...)

Leaving aside the other senses of *hausen* and concentrating on 1. (Wi, P/C),
we see that either only the verbal component "to live" is rendered (P/C,
HC), or completely inaccurate would-be equivalents are offered (Wi),
which if inserted in an English translation could only lead to error.

Focal in *hausen* is not merely the fact of having accommodation, but
above all the *assessment* of the living conditions, whereby the speaker consciously tries to provoke an *emotional* response from the reader. The exact
nature of the conditions referred to and the type of response required can
only be deduced from the function of the item *hausen* in the *text as a whole*:
In the prison text from the *Süddeutsche Zeitung* the element of overcrowd-
ing was focal, while in the case of the moorland cottage an appropriate
translation might run: "...where simple moorland peasants had their hum-
ble homes."

What is important for the translator is the insight that the above rendering — like nearly all literary translation and most other translation outside technical terminology — cannot be taken straight from the dictionary. Certainly the dictionary, both monolingual and bilingual, is an essential tool for the translator, but it should not be understood as an automatic supplier of a kind of ready-made coin that fits neatly into some imagined "slot" in the text. This statement makes clear what was described earlier as the dynamic tension of "word against text," whereby the dictionary indicates the unmarked norm, the basic potential which the translator as writer can use in creating his text as a coherent and organic whole.

3.5.1 *Interlingual relationships*

Up to now the emphasis has been clearly on the concrete text rather than on the abstract system, as is only natural in a study on translation. This does not mean however that the language system can be ignored as something irrelevant to translating. On the contrary, insights into language systems — as provided by contrastive linguistics — could provide a valuable frame of reference for the translator in constructing his text. This chapter will therefore close with a brief account of how lexicology, lexicography and translation studies could be coordinated and integrated so as to lead to such a frame of reference.

It was pointed out in 1.4 above that the results of Contrastive Linguistics have up to now been meagre for translation, that the potential has not as yet been realized. The reason is that the approach has either been too abstract or that the material has been too limited: in the place of rather myopic studies of isolated items (such as characterizes much of the work in contrastive semantics, cf. Snell-Hornby 1983:17), extensive analyses are necessary which admit realization in a context.

As far as the translator is concerned, important differentiations must be made, firstly concerning the methods of semantic analysis, and secondly concerning the term *equivalence* within contrastive linguistics and lexicography.

For many years the accepted method of investigating lexemes was that of *formalized componential analysis*.[24] This was the reductionist "checklist method" based on binary opposites, as was illustrated in 1.3.1 above with the example *bachelor*. Stolze (1982:78) quite rightly points out that for this method only semantic fields were analyzed which referred to concrete objects or actions which could be reduced to distinctive features, while abstract concepts were avoided. A celebrated example of a field successfully analyzed by this binary method are the verbs of cooking. For abstract concepts, especially those linked with tradition and culture, for words expressing perception and evaluation, especially those linked with social norms, the formalized method has proved itself completely unsuitable. This does not however mean that such lexemes cannot be analyzed at all; only the theoretical approach and the methods need to be changed. For such lexemes I have already presented a non-formalized method of *descriptive analysis* (Snell-Hornby 1983) based on a similar concept of prototype or focus as has been presented here. Bierod (1982) has contrasted the two methods, distinguishing between *formalisierte Merkmalanalyse* and *beschreibende Komponentenanalyse*. The results of her study show that the second method, which — as was briefly shown above on the basis of *hausen* admits realization in a context, is undoubtedly of more use to the translator.

In the discussion in 1.2.3 above we rejected the term *equivalence* as a basic concept for translation studies. It is more suitably employed in the field of contrastive linguistics, which investigates areas of convergence and points of divergence at the level of the language-system. Even here however it should be used with caution. As a basic guiding factor in contrastive lexicology — and certainly in the theoretical discussion on bilingual lexicography — a more open approach might be adopted based on the principle of *varying interlingual relationships*, some of which involve some kind of equivalence.

As a fundamental principle we may say that the simplest interlingual relationship — where the term *equivalence* is still justified — exists at the level of *terminology* and *nomenclature*, though even here reservations are called for (cf. Schmitt 1986 and Arntz 1986). The most complex relationships are connected with *dynamic* factors described in 3.5 above, especially perception, subjective evaluation and sociocultural norms, while little or no relationship (up to now called "*nil-equivalence*")[25] exists at the level of *realia* and *culture-bound elements*, with various stages of gradation in between.

Here too we are thinking in terms of prototypical concepts, admitting blend-forms and overlappings, and not in terms of clearly delimited box-like categories. With this in mind, we can distinguish five basic groups of prototypes:

1. *Terminology/Nomenclature*
   e.g. oxygen: Sauerstoff
   reproduktionsfähige Vorlage: camera-ready copy

2. *Internationally known items and sets*
   e.g. Saturday: Sonnabend/Sonntag
   typewriter: Schreibmaschine
   but: to type: mit der Maschine schreiben, tippen

3. *Concrete objects, basic activities, stative adjectives*
   e.g. chair: Stuhl, Sessel
   cook, boil: kochen
   technical: technisch, fachlich, Fach-

4. *Words expressing perception and evaluation, often linked to sociocultural norms*
   e.g. billow, foreboding, gleam, bleak, nag
   keifen, kitschig, gemütlich

5. *Culture-bound elements*
   e.g. haggis, wicket, drugstore
   Pumpernickel, Privatdozent, Sechseläuten.

Such a differentiated approach to interlingual relationships based on prototypes, semantic fields and description (cf. Snell-Hornby 1983) would not only affect work in contrastive semantics (which up to now has invariably been based on some kind of prescriptive equivalence model), but would by necessity revolutionize bilingual lexicography (cf. Zgusta 1984 and Kromann et al. 1984), which up to now has been atomistic in its treatment of words, working strictly from A to Z. A differentiated approach would also lead to differentiated structuring of the dictionary article, which up to now has consisted necessarily of foreign language "equivalents" of the type exemplified above. In our view, equivalence in the strict sense of the term is limited to Group 1 as listed above, and bilingual technical dictionaries of this kind will profitably continue in alphabetical form with foreign language equivalents. Otherwise our list shows a gradual transition from more or less approximate "equivalence" in Group 2 via "equivalence with discrimination" (Group 3) on to "partial overlapping" (Group 4) and definition (Group 5). This should be reflected in the structure of the articles, whereby in the case of more complex, multi-dimensional semantic structures, the traditional alphabetical arrangement might well be supplemented by a presentation in contrastive semantic fields, to which the main body of the dictionary would act as index (cf. Snell-Hornby 1983). The demand for a dictionary of synonyms meeting the needs of professional translators is frequently heard (cf. Senn 1986:83), and it clearly reflects the necessity to integrate the three levels of system (prototype, semantic field), norm (description of unmarked lexical usage) and text (marked usage in concrete expression) which have been pointed out in this study. It is important however to be aware that these levels are by no means identical. The early work of such a distinguished linguist as Wandruszka for example, was ultimately of little use for translation theory because he equated comparisons of individual translated items with a comparison of language systems (Wandruszka 1969, 1971, see discussion of this in Snell-Hornby 1983:239ff.), whereas paradoxically his later work on the phenomenon of language (e.g. 1979, 1985), which does not work at the level of the word or the item, is of more immediate relevance to the translator. Changes in method such as those required by Senn however, will demand changes in thinking — a utopian aim in both translation practice and lexicography, both of them areas not only bound by tradition, but often even paralyzed by unquestioned fixed ideas and prejudices. But changes would seem to be necessary if semantic theory, lexicography and translation are to be usefully combined.

Notes

1. This is effectively illustrated by examples taken from his experiences in fire prevention engineering, as with sometimes fatal reactions to "empty gasoline drums," "spun limestone" and "pool of water" (Whorf 1963:135f.) described in the essay "The relation of habitual thought and behavior" (1963:134-159).

2. The early history of the Prague Circle is described in Vachek 1966:137ff.

3. The relation between text-linguistics and translation theory is discussed in detail by Stolze (1982:55-74), who shows effectively that by no means all approaches to text-linguistics are relevant for translation studies.

4. Cf. Hönig 1986, and see too Wilss 1977a, Thiel 1981, Reiss 1984 and Nord 1991. Textual analysis is particularly important in translator training, as the professional translator, usually working under time pressure, needs to draw rapidly from the fund of knowledge and experience gained in this way.

5. Cf. Stolze 1982: 286ff. for a discussion of "Isotopieebenen im Text" (after Greimas 1974). Our concept of *field-progression* is developed from Stolze's analysis.

6. This sense of foreboding is borne out in the stories that follow (which frequently culminate in the death of the main protagonist), and is hence an essential element for the translation.

7. These were Swiss students of English at the University of Zürich, German students of Translation Studies at the University of Heidelberg, and Austrian students of Translation Studies at the University of Innsbruck.

8. This involvement of the reader is made possible by the flexible use of *you* in English (contrast the far more specific modes of address in German, as discussed in 3.4 below), as against the much more limited *du*-form in German. It was generally agreed in the groups that this is a problem for which there is no simple solution.

9. Ria Vanderauwera (1985) has investigated the poor response to Dutch novellas translated into English; such reactions might have been anticipated had suitable analyses been carried out.

10. The idea of using Fillmore's scenes-and-frames concept in translator training came from Mia Vannerem. This section is an adapted English version of my contribution to Vannerem and Snell-Hornby 1986.

11. By this Fillmore means the differing perspectives as in the verbs *buy*, *sell* and *cost* (cf. Fillmore 1977:59).

12. For this purpose phrases and conventions were studied in comparable British newspapers with liberal and progressive leanings (e.g. *The Guardian. The Times*).

13. For an explanation of the term *vehicle* (or *Vorgangsträger* as in Leisi 1975), see Snell-Hornby 1983.

14. This concept of "dynamic tension" within language and the interdependence of levels can also be traced back to the Prague School (cf. Halliday 1976 and Vachek 1966).

15. These are familiar notices in West German public telephone booths.

16. Cf. CED definitions: *Forbid*: To prohibit (a person) in a forceful or authoritative manner (from doing something or having something). *Prohibit*: To forbid by law or other authority.

17. In Switzerland the modal verb *dürfen* was occasionally found in notices issued by university authorities or private organizations (hence not involving direct legal consequences). In Germany and Austria modals were not found in public notices.

18. This was basic to the dogma of early structuralism, behaviourism (cf. Bloomfield 1933) and transformational generative grammar.

19. In other instances Leisi does draw parallels with English and American linguists. See his comments on the operational definition of meaning in Leisi 1973:35f.

20. This is a small sub-section included in the grammar to point out the "Semantic sub-classification of adjectives," but the link between grammar and meaning is not followed to its logical conclusion.

21. The needs of the user have only very recently been considered by lexicographers at all (cf. Cowie, 1987), and up to now only the needs of the language learner, not the translator, have been examined in detail.

22.   Cf. Rose's comments on this (Rose 1981:35f.).

23.   P/C enters the English version under *Proletarier*, but this still presupposes the ability to make the connection described in the first step listed here.

24.   Cf. my comments in Snell-Hornby 1983:63ff.

25.   Cf. Kade's typology of equivalence-types discussed in 1.2.3; in effect Kade is operating in terms of contrastive lexicology and not translation theory.

4. From special language to literary translation

This chapter is an attempt to relativize some of the clear tendencies that have emerged on fundamental issues in translation. The most striking of these is the constant *swing of orientation* from source to target text. The second is the recent rejection of the *evaluative* approach in literary translation studies in favour of a purely *descriptive* one. The third, an issue mainly involving linguistically oriented translatology, is the shift of emphasis from the formal aspect of the text as an isolated fragment of language to the *function* of the translation as part of a broader *sociocultural background*. In all of the more recent theories, a clear choice is made in favour of the function of the target text as part of the target culture (Vermeer, Hönig and Kussmaul, Toury, Hermans), while opinions are still dived as to whether translation theory should be evaluative (Hönig and Kussmaul) or descriptive (Toury, Hermans). The question is however justified as to whether such absolute and sweeping statements should be made at all, if in fact a differentiation should not be made according to the *type of text* and the factors arising in its translation. Again abandoning the polarized dichotomy in favour of the spectrum with its areas of dynamic tension, I should like to present the hypothesis that the emphasis and orientation should *vary* according to the constellation of text-type, stylistic profile and extent of non-linguistic constraints. The argument will be supported by reference to translations covering the range of problems involved.

4.1 The status of the source text

At the heart of the recent translation theories lies what Vermeer has called the "dethroning of the source text". This he applied to all types of translation; Hönig and Kussmaul have demonstrated it on the basis of non-literary texts, and the Netherlands scholars demand it for literary translation. To my knowledge, no comparative analysis has as yet been made as to the status of the source text in relationship to the text-type.

Common to the work of all recent translation theorists from Paepcke to Newmark and Holz-Mänttäri is the emphasis on the *situation* of the source text and the *function* of the translation: "Sprache als Text in einer Situation, als Teil einer Kultur mit einer bestimmten Funktion" (Language as text-in-situation, as part of a culture with a definite function of its own) is how I have formulated it (Snell-Hornby 1986:26). We shall now examine the relation between situation and source-text type on the one hand, and function and target-text type on the other, and then discuss them with specific reference to the four texts reproduced with their translations in the Appendix.

None of the translation theorists quoted here so far has doubted the crucial influence of the background situation upon the text. This stands in direct contrast to the conclusion drawn by Roland Barthes (1966:54) that literary language, as against ordinary language, has no situation.

Barthes creates a clear distinction — a dichotomy — between the literary work (*l'oeuvre*) with its "prophetic" openness, its "pure ambiguity" on the one hand, and "practical language," which is always embedded in a situation as recent translation theory understands it, on the other. In his discussion of the reading process, Iser (1976:89ff.) proceeds from a similar starting point: that the "reale Situation" (which formed part of the speech act theory) is not present in a literary text. Iser however takes the argument a good deal further. In a section entitled "Die Situationsbildung fiktionaler Texte" (1976:101-114), he describes the process of *interaction* between reader and text: these are involved in a dynamic situation produced during the reading process which creates the illusion that the fictional action is really taking place. This complements Beaugrande and Dressler's definition of the literary text as one that presents a systematic alternative to the accepted version of the "real world".[1] As a starting point, I would support this premise that a literary text does not exist in a vacuum; while it is not bound to a single, specific situation as is a road sign or a legal contract, it has its own situational relationship to reality. This is created on the one hand through the dynamics of the individual act of reading, as described by Iser, and on the other by virtue of the literary work of art being absorbed into its cultural heritage. Thus a text which is accepted as part of a literary canon assumes a degree of independence and stability as an artist's documentation of perceived or imagined events in a certain time, place and culture, as constantly recreated through interaction in the minds of readers living at another time and/or in another place or culture. Such a relationship to the text, described above (2.4) as *perspective*, may shift according to changes brought about by distance, both spatial and temporal, and changes in cultural values, but it means that the literary work is not, as Barthes seems to suggest, entirely "open": the relationship created between text and reader is always conditioned by some kind of situational or cultural constraint. A third situational dimension can be developed from the alternativity theory put forward by Beaugrande and Dressler, which suggests that a novel, for example, presents an alternative world full of its own situations, hence is itself a system of "texts within a text." Obvious examples of such micro-texts would be the Seven Commandments in *Animal Farm* or Mr Micawber's letters in *David Copperfield*; these are never interpreted in isolation, but are integrated by the reader into his global understanding of the novel as a whole, whereby a relationship is created — be it irony, parody, causality or contingence — between the micro-text and the textual system.[2]

Looking at the function of the translation in the target culture, we see that a similar picture arises. The text of a public directive is the direct product of a specific situation, and its translation has a prescribed function to fulfil for specific target-language readers, fully in keeping with the tenets of modern translation theories. The literary translation on the other hand seems at first sight to be as far removed from prescribed functions as is the literary text from a specific situation. Once again however, the literary translation is by no means without any function at all, and here too we can identify three functional dimensions. One is the function of intra-textual coherence: the "alternative world" provides its own inner functions for its system or cosmos of micro-texts, these too being integrated into the reading process to form a message "received" and interpreted by the reader of the translation, thus creating the second dimension of "functional interaction" similar to the one described by Iser.[3] And thirdly, underlying the literary translator's work is the wish — or the publisher's commission — to recreate and hence to perpetuate a work of fiction or a work of art within a given target context, that is, for readers at a given time, in a given language and culture; in this sense the literary translation is as much an act of communication as any other translation. Only rarely however does the literary translation attain the stability of an original work (the Schlegel-Tieck translations of Shakespeare are such rarities); it is hardly ever handed down from one generation to another as a work of art in itself, more often it becomes ossified as merely a dated text. In other words, it loses its communicative function as a work of literature within a continually shifting cultural system. This explains why the need so often arises to create new translations of literary works.

In some cases — these are unfortunately still all too rare — the translator explains the intended function of the specific text he has created in a preface or appendix; this was the case with Christian Enzenberger's translation of Alice in Wonderland.[4] In other cases, publishers have specific aims and a specific type of reader in mind for a translation they commission, thus making the literary work as "functional" as any newspaper article. This was the case with Josef Thanner's translations of Dickens: instructions were received from the publisher to avoid long sentences or complicated syntax and to make the text accessible to the German reader with average education.[5] Particularly in the case of Dickens, one wonders how such instructions are compatible with the richness and sophistication of the original prose style. Usually however, the literary translator gives no indication of his intention, and publishers' constraints remain unknown: it is a hallmark of the prototypical literary translation that it is assumed to stand as a valid full-scale representative of the original in a foreign culture (see Beaugrande 1978:14 and cf. p. 21 above); with this awesome function a literary translation is bound to have shortcomings and faultfinders somewhere.

This differentiation between the literary text on the one hand and the public directive on the other as prototype of the "pragmatic" text is not however presented as the type of dichotomy we have rejected in an integrated approach to translation. On the contrary, the observations made above are again to be understood dynamically within the concept of the spectrum with its relative and shifting focal points, the prototypes with merging and overlapping elements. Taking the cline from special language to literary translation as a starting point, we can therefore formulate the following tentative hypotheses:

(1) the more "specialized" or "pragmatic" the source text, the more closely it is bound to a single, specific situation, and the easier it is to define the function of its translation;

(2) the more specific the situation and the more clearly defined the function, the more target-oriented the translation is likely to be;

(3) the more "literary" a text (whether original or translation), the more both "situation" and "function" depend on reader activation;

(4)   the more "literary" a translation, the higher is the status of the source text as a work of art using the medium of language.

These hypotheses will now be demonstrated and tested on the basis of the four texts reproduced with their translations in the Appendix; three of them are from the author's own workshop. Text A is the original German version of the guidelines sent by Niemeyer Publishers to their authors on how to present manuscripts for the series *Lexicographica. Series Maior*; the English translation was commissioned by the publishers in 1986. Text B is the original English version of the Second Circular for the EURALEX International Congress held in Zürich in 1986; the translation is the version for German-speaking participants. Text C is taken from an anthology of essays written in German to commemorate the 2000th anniversary (1985) of the foundation of the city of Augsburg; the translation, commissioned by the publishers, is intended for distribution in the English-speaking world. Text D is the opening of Dylan Thomas' *A Child's Christmas in Wales*, with its translation by Erich Fried.

Text A

1.   *Situation of source text*

The sender (Niemeyer Publishers Tübingen) is clearly defined, the addressees (German-speaking authors) form a restricted, homogeneous group (academics). The circumstances are likewise clearly defined and restricted; the text consists solely of instructions on the presentation of manuscripts for a specialized series of academic publications.

2.   *Function of target text*

The same sender issues basically the same instructions to a much broader, more heterogeneous group of academics. These may be native speakers of English (e.g. American, British, Australian) or speakers of other languages writing in English as the lingua franca of linguistics (e.g. Poles, Egyptians, Israelis). The aim is to ensure that these authors submit camera-ready manuscripts meeting certain standard requirements as specified in the German text. This aim will determine the wording of the translation, which is thus *fully oriented* towards target function.

3.   *Status of the source text*

As a purely functional text as basis for a target-oriented translation, the text is merely a means towards an end.

4. Conclusion

The translation will be influenced by the *change in situation* between SL addressees (as members of a technologically advanced industrial society) and TL addressees (many of whom are unlikely to have easy access to equipment specified in the source text).

Text B

1. Situation of source text

As the Second Circular for the EURALEX International Congress held in Zürich in 1986, the text is embedded in a specific, temporary, very clearly defined situation. The sender (Congress Organizer) is defined by name, the group of addressees (potential Congress participants) is however more diffuse than with (source) Text A. English is used here as a lingua franca for both native speakers and any other participant in a position to *understand* it. There is a certain homogeneity in the group in that all are foreigners to Switzerland (many are from overseas), hence likely to be unfamiliar with certain procedures (e.g. the specified method of booking accommodation).

2. Function of target text

The German version of the same circular aims at giving the *necessary* information to potential participants from German-speaking countries (or those parts of Europe where German is a first foreign language). The *perspective* changes for the target text in that familiarity with procedures, customs and locality can to a certain extent be presupposed. The text is *fully oriented* towards target function.

3. Status of source text

The English original is the *pilot version* for three translations (French, German and Italian), all of which are individually oriented to their respective target audience, as is the German. From the *communicative* point of view however, the English text aims at combining clarity of information with a subdued friendliness of tone, both of which should be preserved in all three translations.

4. Conclusion

While the communicative tone will be preserved in the German translation, the change of perspective makes some items of the English text superfluous (e.g. the request not to pay by cheque, 1.49), while other information (such as the section on transport) needs to be adapted.

Text C

1. Situation of source text

The text consists of the opening paragraphs of an essay in a volume commemorating the bimillenary of the city of Augsburg in 1985. The anthology aims at giving an account of the many facets still perceptible in the history of Augsburg and characteristic of the city of today, but the information is presented throughout in a strikingly positive light, in the present case even with rapturous enthusiasm. The topic of the essay is the musical tradition in Augsburg since the First World War as demonstrated by the conductors who have worked there. The communicative aspects of the situation differ from both previous texts, where the sender was clearly defined by the specific situational role (publisher, organizer) and communicated directly to a particular group of addressees in this situational capacity only. Here there is no such direct communication, and we are approaching the more open author-reader relationship that characterizes publications for the open market. Aspects of a specifically German socio-cultural background are prominent: the author is given authority by the mention of her academic title; the city is vested with cultural prestige by terms like "Dirigentenwunder" and "Opernstadt" (l.1) and titles such as "Städtischer Kapellmeister" (l.25) and "Operndirektor" (l.52). Perspective plays an important part here too: a German author discusses aspects of German history over the last 70 years and includes phrases like "die zwölf Jahre des 'Tausendjährigen Reichs'" (1.48f.) and "'unbelastete' Musiker" (1.74), which implicitly define the type of reader who is addressed: the specifically German reader who can understand the implications of such phrases without any further explanation.

2. *Function of target text*

The English version of the anthology, as specified by the commissioner of the translation, was intended for the "English-speaking world" in general, but in particular for those speakers of English (such as former US soldiers) already familiar with Augsburg. This changes the perspective of the text considerably. Firstly, the native German reader, on home ground, is replaced by the foreigner, whether or not he or she has been temporarily resident in Augsburg. Historical aspects of the text must be expressed accordingly. Sociocultural factors are of primary importance: for example, the type of reader addressed will have a different relationship to operatic tradition — he will expect a more sober tone, if he is to take the article seriously, and he is unlikely to appreciate the full significance of the "opernbesessenen Bäckermeisterin" (1.4). Such items will need to be aligned to the primary function of the target text: to present the topic in such a way that the English-speaking reader is positively impressed by the musical personalities and achievements described.

3. *Status of source text*

Given the above function, we see that the source text becomes little more than a draft for adaptation. Some points (titles, historical details) need clarifying, others lose relevance.

4. *Conclusion*

While the overall factual information in the text must be presented undistorted in the English version, incidental details need to be tested for relevance in the translation, and the communicative tone will be adapted to those expectations predictable in the target culture.

Text D

1. *Situation of source text*

The text is the opening of the impressionistic sketch "A Child's Christmas in Wales," written in 1945[6] by the Welsh poet Dylan Thomas (1914-1953). Whatever autobiographical features may be recognizable, the text, far from being a factual account, is highly imaginative and atmospheric, and complies with the definition of a literary text as presented by Beaugrande and Dressler. The first two paragraphs are reproduced here, each representing a slightly different perspective: the first, written mainly in the past tense, portrays the introductory fragments of childhood recollections from the perspective of the adult; the second paragraph, written in the present tense, activates the perspective of the child reliving images and experiences presented as concrete items. The text has the form of a monologue: the narrator recalls his own childhood without any specified reader orientation.

2. *Function of target text*

The text was translated into German by Erich Fried (b.1921), himself a distinguished poet and a renowned translator of English literature (e.g. Shakespeare, T.S. Eliot, Graham Greene) into German. He settled in London, where he emigrated in 1938. The edition used here is the two-language version with illustrations published by Arche, Zürich as "Eines Kindes Weihnacht in Wales. Eine Erzählung Englisch-Deutsch." The two texts are printed parallel to each other, the English on the left, the German on the right. These combined factors indicate that this edition is intended for the cultured German-speaking reader who is able to compare the two versions, while the presentation of the volume, with the whimsical illustrations by Robert Wyss, shows that this publication has the aesthetic aim of pleasing the reader; it is not a book intended for scientific study.

3. *Status of source text*

As emerges from the above, the two texts are given equal status; each can act as the valid representative of the other for the reader who chooses to compare and contrast. The German title may give the translated text (and the target reader) prominence, but the parallel presentation keeps the awareness alive that this is one poet's version of another poet's text.

4. *Conclusion*

As text comparison is part of the basic intention of the edition, we are fully justified in analyzing the translation critically as a literary text in its own right and comparing the analysis to that of the original. Important for the analysis is the change of perspective brought about by the element *Wales* in the title: unlike the source text, the German translation refers to customs and events which are *foreign* to the target reader.

In all three aspects discussed here — background situation, function of translation and status of source text — we can indeed detect a progression according to text-type: the further we progress from the prototype of the specialized and pragmatic text, the less tangible the background situation becomes, the more open is the function of the translation and the higher the status of the source text.

Precisely these conclusions have also been reached by Marilyn Gaddis Rose (1981:33), who refers to what she calls the "autonomy spectrum:"

> All of these divisions point to the autonomy spectrum. The two poles here are source text autonomy versus target audience needs. The gradations along the spectrum mark both the translator's relation to his material and the translation's relation to its audience. The translator, we might say, can go from reverence to reference; the translation, from presentation to adaptation.

4.2 The factor of style

Style is nominally an important factor in translation, but there are few detailed or satisfactory discussions of its role within translation theory. In their definitions of translation quoted in 1.2.3 above, both Nida and Wilss put style on a par with meaning or content. In Reiss 1971, Wilss 1977 and Koller 1979, references to aspects of style in translation are frequent, and Stolze devotes a complete section (1982:300ff.) to the question of style. In all cases however, the discussion is linked to specific items or examples, and no coherent theoretical approach is attempted. In the recent theories of Vermeer and Holz-Mänttäri the problem of style recedes perceptibly into the background: in Holz-Mänttäri 1984 it is barely mentioned,[7] and in Reiss and Vermeer 1984 the topic is limited to brief references to the general need for a "Stiltheorie" in translation (1984:22, 219). Up to now this has remained a desideratum.

The concept of style, described by David Lodge as "surely one of the most vexed terms in the vocabulary of literary criticism" (1966: 49), has in recent decades gained new impetus within the field of stylistics,[8] especially by linguists applying it to various aspects of language. One classic investigation of the style of everyday English, Crystal and Davy 1969, was developed into a model for translation quality assessment by House (1977) and was also instrumental in Hönig's model of text analysis for translation (1986). In neither case however has the model been developed further into a theory of style for translation. Two studies of the style of literary language have been presented by Leech, one on poetry (1969), the other on prose fiction (Leech and Short 1981). Especially the latter work adopts an approach which shows some striking similarities with the one presented in this study: it is both pragmatic and pluralistic, and owes much of its thought-content to the theories of Halliday (whose concept of the cline formed part of the theoretical basis for the diagrams presented in 1.4 and 3.4 above). The relevant components of Leech and Short's theoretical model, which proceeds from the broad concept of style as a system of *choices* within language use (1981:10ff.), are listed here as a starting point for a theoretical approach to style in translation:

(1)   The multilevel approach to style (1981: 34) is based on the plurality of *semantics*, *syntax* and the physical properties of the text (*graphology* for written, *phonology* for spoken language (1981:121).

(2)   This "plurality of coding levels" is correlated with a *plurality of text functions* (Halliday) (1981:136).[9]

(3)   Style may be measured *quantitatively* by determining the *frequency* of stylistic features.[10] (1981:42ff.).

(4)   Salient in Leech's approach is the notion of *foregrounding*[11] or *artistically motivated deviation* from the norms of the linguistic code (1981:48). This may be *qualitative* (e.g. a breach of some rule or convention in the language) or *quantitative* (i.e. deviance from an expected frequency).

(5)   Leech and Short differentiate between *transparent style*, which shows the meaning of the text easily and directly (1981:19), and *opaque style*, where the meaning of the text is obscured by means of foregrounding and its interpretation is hence obstructed (1981:29). Transparent style focusses on the content expressed, opaque style on the *medium of language* in its own right (1981:29).

Two basic focal points emerge from this list, both of which are connected with topics already dealt with here: firstly, the principle of the multilevel approach to style (cf. 3.2 above), and secondly the phenomenon of the *norm* (cf. 2.3). Both of these will now be developed and applied to translation.

In our discussion of text analysis (3.2) the emphasis lay on the macro-level of text-structure; similarly, the discussion of text status (4.1) was concerned with macro-elements such as overall situation and text function. A stylistic analysis, concerned with choices in language use, continues this "top-down procedure" and leads it down into the micro-levels. Beginning with *syntax*, a stylistic analysis will consider such points as sentence *structure* (paratactic, coordinating, hypotactic) and length; *arrangement* of information (focus and stress); structure and frequency of *noun phrases* and *verb phrases*, especially in relation to each other (nominal and verbal style). This leads us to the level of semantics and lexis: continuing the macro-concept of field progression described in 3.2, the analysis concentrates on the semantic properties of lexical items (cf. 3.5 above), word-formation, and especially the usage of multiple dimension (cf. 2.4) as with metaphor, word-play and pun. This is also the level of the classical rhetorical devices familiar in traditional literary analysis. The lowest level concerns elements *within* the words such as alliteration and assonance (this corresponds to, but is not identical with, Leech and Short's level of graphology and phonology).

Problems of *norm* are crucial in the study of style, and the language norm is one aspect of style that has received detailed attention in translation theory (cf. Wilss 1977; Koller 1979; Reiss 1971; Hönig and Kussmaul 1982; Stolze 1982 and others). Leech and Short follow the traditional trend in linguistics by presenting a binary approach: *keeping* the norm on the one hand and *deviating* from it on the other. This is the point where our approach differs from theirs: we have already discussed the concept of norm (2.3) and its *creative extension*, which differs essentially from deviation as anomaly. The language norm is in fact supremely flexible, it offers potential for creativity within the possibilities of the language system. This is of crucial importance for the translator, especially the literary translator.

This can be illustrated on the microlevel of semantic analysis by two dimensions I have called *opaque* and *transparent* style (Snell-Hornby 1983). The terminology was taken from Ullmann's discussion of motivation in word-formation (1973: 12ff.), and it is purely coincidental that Leech and Short have adopted precisely the same terms in their study of style — or more accurately, it would be coincidental if they were not pointing out a very similar phenomenon as that discussed in Snell-Hornby 1983, for which the metaphors *opaque* and *transparent* are eminently suitable. Leech and Short's approach is stylistic, mine was primarily semantic, and it seems to offer a more precise explanation for stylistic opacity than does the appeal to foregrounding (and hence deviance). Concentrating on the lexical level, we can say that in transparent style the meaning of a word is elucidated by its context. If we broke down the lexemes into semantic components,[12] we would register a high degree of redundancy and reinforcement; collocation rules are faithfully applied, verbs and connectives are used in lucid and logical relation to each other. This is the language of straight traditional writing and of light fiction, as exemplified by the following brief passage from Christopher Isherwood's novel *Mr Norris Changes Trains*:

> He was *extremely nervous*. His delicate white hand *fiddled incessantly* with the signet ring on his little finger; his *uneasy* blue eyes kept *squinting rapid glances* into the corridor. (15)

Here the general picture of extreme anxiety is constantly reinforced: *extremely nervous* by *fiddled incessantly*, *uneasy blue eyes* and *squinting rapid glances*. Semantic congruence is observed for verb and participants:[13] *hand* and *fiddle*; *eye*, *squint* and *glance*; and the objects described are in perfect compatibility with each other: *delicate white hand*, *signet ring*, *little finger*. The basic characteristics of transparent style are therefore semantic reinforcement and coordination, and for translation purposes it is not irrelevant that the sense of individual lexemes is often deducible from the context in which they are embedded. In opaque style on the other hand, words are not elucidated by the context in this way; on the contrary, they are often used so idiosyncratically that the reader has to be familiar with all the semantic implications of the lexeme concerned before he can appreciate its impact on the text. In many cases of opaque style, the focal elements of the lexemes are preserved, while their peripheral components do not coincide with accepted usage as in the unmarked dictionary norm. This type of writing is characteristic of Lawrence Durrell, as in this example from *Balthazar*:

> Soon the cicadas will bring in their *crackling* music, background to the shepherd's dry flute among the rocks. The *scrambling* tortoise and the lizard are our only companions. (16)

Normally *crackle* describes the sound made by dry twigs or fire, not that made by a live creature, and it does not collocate with music; the focal element, a rapid succession of dry brittle sounds, is however retained here. Similarly *scramble* typically takes a human agent, whereby arms and legs are involved: in the above example the focal elements of effort and hasty, disorganized movement are however retained. Obviously the more obscure opaque style, where there is more danger of misunderstanding the text and of introducing incongruous elements in the target language, presents greater difficulty for the translator than does transparent style, and where the pitfalls are recognized and actual errors avoided, the translation is usually made transparent. This is often the cause of what reviewers like to call "Verflachung" or "lack of stylistic contour" in a translation. The authorized German translation of *Balthazar* by G. von Uslar and M. Carlsson offers the following rendering of the above example:

> Bald werden die Zikaden ihre *knarrende* Musik anstimmen, Hintergrund für die klare Flötenstimme des Schafhirten zwischen den Felsen. Die *schwerfällige* Schildkröte und die Eidechse sind unsere einzigen Gefährten. (10)

In the case of "knarrende Musik" the opaque element has been well recreated in the German text, while "die schwerfällige Schildkröte" ("the clumsy tortoise") has been "flattened" to form transparent style. This means that incongruities in the German are avoided, but that the language becomes banal and loses elements of depth and subtlety.

As the above examples show, the distinction between opaque and transparent style highlights the subtle relationship between norm and text discussed in 2.3 above: while transparent style clings to the unmarked norm and faithfully observes accepted usage, opaque style represents the creative extension of the norm through subtle exploitation of language potential.

4.2.1 Style and convention

Both the phenomenon of opaque style as discussed above and the concept of foregrounding as artistically motivated deviation apply essentially to literary language, to the individual style of the creative writer. Looking at the other end of the spectrum of text-types, we see that our conception of style needs further explanation and delimitation.

Style is understood in this study as it is presented by Leech and Short, as a system of choices in language use by an *individual* writer. It is not used as in Crystal and Davy 1969 to include the social level of the group, the form of language associated with certain social situations (such as the language of religion or newspaper reporting[14]).

The question arises however, whether the writer as an individual artist has the same status in any kind of text. The answer is that the more specialized the text, and the more specific the situation, the more the individual style recedes to make way for *group convention*. In a special language text the circle of readers and the relation to the non-linguistic world are limited and prescribed. An important feature of the prototypical special language text is that, however "opaque" the language may appear to the non-initiated layman, within the circle of designated addressees the meaning must be transparent. This applies for both the scientific report and the legal document. In this case, the transparency is not only a matter of semantic components: it extends to correct and accepted use of special terms and, particularly in the case of legal language, special conventions of syntax. For translation purposes, such conventions can easily be studied and compared in several languages on the basis of parallel texts (cf. 3.4 above).

The tension between this concept of group convention on the one hand and individual style with the concept of the norm as language potential on the other, will now be demonstrated, by means of a multilevel analysis, on the basis of the four texts in the Appendix with their translations; once again we shall proceed from the special language to the literary text.

Text A

1.   *Syntax*

The sentence structure is simple, with occasionally a dependent clause (e.g. 1.3/4, 8/9, 18/19). Verbs are frequently used impersonally in the passive; semantically their content is weak, they are mainly functional. The style is predominantly *nominal*.

2.   *Semantics and lexis*

There is a high proportion of specialized terminology (e.g. *reproduktionsfähige Vorlage* (1.3), *12er- Schritteinteilung* (1.5), *kursive Auszeichnung* (1.23/24)) and such conventionalized phrases as *eingeschobene Beispielsätze* (1.40) and *1-zeilige Schaltung* (1.45/46). A new term, "Tuck" (1.26), has been coined for the purpose of this text; it is explained in lines 27-29.

3.   *Formal text presentation*

Most striking is the numerical presentation and the division of paragraphs into individual spaced items.

4.   *Translation strategies and methods*

For translation purposes the highly conventionalized source text was compared with two English parallel texts (one American and one British), the *LSA Style Sheet* and a style sheet circulated privately for a specific publication (both reproduced in the Appendix). A syntactic and semantic analysis of these parallel texts shows:

(1)   While the English texts also favour simple syntax, the impersonal passives are replaced by *imperative forms* and modal verbs such as *should* or *must*.

(2)   English has its own conventionalized expressions corresponding to the German ones (though not their word-for-word renderings): viz. "single/double spacing," "72 characters at 12 pitch," etc.

Other fixed expressions of this kind were found in specialized dictionaries and by reference to a terminological data bank. In English convention the concept of spacing is not as differentiated as in German; the problem mentioned in 1.25/26 of the German text does not therefore arise, the term *Tuck* was found to be misleading rather than enlightening for the reader of the English translation and hence omitted. Similarly, the formal numbering system, while frequently used in academic writings, is not standard practice in English publication guidelines, and was not used in the English translation, though the spacing system of the original was retained.

Text B

1.   *Syntax, semantics and lexis*

The conference circular is another conventionalized text-type, but lacks the standardized special-language terminology observed in Text A and hence approaches the pragmatic text prototype of general language usage. Given the double (informative and communicative) function observed above, two clear tendencies can be identified in both syntax and lexis:

(1)   a large number of impersonal constructions are used (*are ... advanced* (l.1), *is sent* (l.4/5), *is enclosed* (l.8), *will be presented* (l.9), *is not envisaged* (l.24), *will be mounted* (l.29) and many others), along with set, conventionalized phrases (as under the heading *Cost*).

(2)   a direct approach to the reader is maintained through the personal pronoun (especially from l.47 onwards), the use of the imperative (*Please pay* (l.48), *Please note* (l.55), *Please contact* (l.70) and others) and identification of the situational role of the addressee as *participant* (l.58, 79/80, 85; cf. 3.4 above). Particularly passages with this communicative function provide scope for free stylistic expression.

2.   *Formal text presentation*

The text is divided into sections with subheadings for easy reference.

3. *Translation strategies and methods*

Parallel texts are also useful for the text-type "Conference Circular," but for the wording of the translation they provide a general frame of reference rather than a model for direct imitation. German conventions for conference circulars favour both the use of the passive and function verbs such as *zur Verfügung stehen* (1.32), *betragen* (1.36) and *erfolgen* (1.48). As we saw in 3.4 however, the direct approach to the reader by means of identification, personal pronoun and imperative is less customary in German than in English (cf. *Es empfiehlt sich* (1.62) and *Es wird empfohlen* (1.81/82) of the German version). For the more individually worded passages with stronger communicative function at the end, authentic comments were used (cf. "The city itself is notoriously difficult to negotiate" (1.76/77) and "... ist der Verkehrssalat berüchtigt" (1.79/80).

Text C

1. *Syntax, semantics and lexis*

This text shows elements of both free, individualistic expression and conventional cliché (e.g. "souveräne Beherrschung" (1.50/51), "ausgedehnte Wagner-Praxis" (1.53/54), "von höchst imponierendem Können" (1.24)). On the syntactic level, the highly complex sentence structures in the first paragraph are conspicuous, and the entire passage is characterized by frequent emphasis and initial focussing through fronting ("Ohne Wunder..." (1.22), "Aus Chemnitz..." (1.50), "Aus Bayreuth..." (1.53), "Als starke Persönlichkeit..." (1.61) etc.). On the semantic level the most salient features are the word-play on *Wunder* (1.1-22) and the density of dynamic adjectives with extremely positive evaluation (*höchst imponierend* (1.24), *hervorragend* (1.34), *souverän* (1.50), *grundsolide* (1.57), *feinnervig* (1.78/79), *künstlerisch integer* (1.79) and many others). Such adjectives confirm the impression that the text tends more to rhetoric than concrete information; further evidence is provided by the rhetorical questions in the first paragraph accentuating the already convoluted syntax.

2. *Formal text presentation*

There is less formal structuring of the text than was the case so far, despite the subheadings pointing out the significance of the various musical personalities discussed.

3. *Translation strategies and methods*

We have noted that both the syntactic complexity and the verbal acrobatics with the item *Wunder* are used as rhetorical devices by way of introducing the topic; neither add vital information, on the contrary, the elements of *Wunder* are taken up so often in the essay itself that it proves repetitive and redundant. A word-for-word English translation with this combination of verbal flourish and irrelevant trivialities would have the effect of cheap showmanship where concrete information is needed, albeit presented in such a way as to impress. The translated text was therefore made more concise and less complex than the German original; the syntax of the opening sentences was simplified and rhetorical devices without a necessary function in the text were eliminated, including the play on *Wunder*. The compound *Dirigentenwunder* in the title was replaced by "Great Maestros" and the salient theme of "tradition" accentuated. The overly positive evaluation in the text was toned down and the clichés reduced.

Text D

1.   *Syntax*

Each of the two paragraphs presented here is a single sentence of 19 and 26 lines, respectively; in quantitative relationship to the average sentence in modern English, this is extremely long, but there is no actual deviation from the rules of English syntax. In the first sentence the distance in time-perspective and the dimness of recollection is accentuated by the complex hypotactic constructions (l.3-8) leading out of the introductory main clause (l.1), and by the series of coordinated constructions dependent on the subordinated *whether* (l.8), which continue for the rest of the sentence.

The next sentence also begins simply with the main clause, upon which there follows a long series of paratactically arranged items: adverbials (l.19-23), three coordinated main clauses (l.23, 24, 25) and a list of items corresponding to the memories which together form the figurative "snowball" (l.20) of Christmas reminiscences (l.26 to end).

Rhythm, focus and stress are all important in these super-sentences, and are accentuated by correlative coordinates (l.1, 5), reiteration through reversal (l.5-8), anticlimax after a long syntactic build-up or stress by opposition (l.43-44).

Bordering on to the lexical and semantic level is the bold extension of the language norm shown in compound adjective phrases, especially in the second paragraph: *ice-edged, fish-freezing waves* (l.24), *baby-burning flames* (l.31), and above all *thimble-hiding musical-chairing blind-man's-buffing party* (l.41-3), where lexical and cultural items gain a new quality by the shift in word-class and the syntactic density.

2.   *Semantics and lexis*

Basically, the lexical items are concrete, simple, everyday and monosyllabic: *snow, ice, jelly, hill, sea, holly, robins, bells, tin-soldiers, party*. A striking characteristic of the text — beside the above-mentioned compound phrases — is however the unusual number of culture-bound items: *mince-pies* (l.11), (Christmas) *pudding* (l.26), *Black Beauty, Little Women* (l.33), the party songs "Pop Goes the Weasel," "Nuts in May" and "Oranges and Lemons" (l.39/40) and many others, which pose considerable difficulties for the translator.

3.   *Formal text presentation*

In accordance with literary conventions, the text has no formal divisions except the arrangement in paragraphs. Each sentence-paragraph is a thematic and syntactic unit in itself.

4.   *Translation critique*

It is a merit of Erich Fried's German version that he has — from the syntactic point of view — done justice to this miniature work of art. His apparent division of each sentence into two is deceptive: in fact he has only converted a pause (semi-colon 1.8; dash 1.32) into a full stop. The syntactic pattern has been convincingly recreated in the German sentence-structure with all its cumulative effect of rhythm, piling up of phrases and convulated but never confusing complexes of dependent clauses. As compound adjective phrases are used more naturally in German than in English, these presented no real problem: not only are the phrases "am Ufer der eisgeränderten, fische-frierenden Wellen" (1.29/30) and "den ganzen Pfänder und Blindekuh spielenden Abend lang" (1.53/54) aesthetically pleasing translations, they are even reinforced in the German version by renderings like "wie ein kalter und kopfüber kollernder Mond" (1.26/27) of simple adjective phrases in English (here: "cold and headlong moon" 1.21/22).

The culture-bound items are not so felicitous: while the German title clearly pinpoints the setting as Wales and the occasion to be "Weihnacht," the reader of the German text is presented with a medley of more or less definable items, from the specifically German *Tannenzweige* (1.32) to the bland everyday dish *Pudding* (1.33); equally heterogeneous are the party songs, which turn into the specifically German "Ein Männlein steht im Walde" (1.51/52), associated, not with Christmas, but with very small children in kindergarten, and an unidentifiable "Orangen und Lemonen." It is for this reason that the German text is less cohesive than the English one. Certainly the culture-bound items present problems with their specific associations which combine to form a certain image of "Christmas" that varies from country to country, but a strategy might well have been developed to create associations in German relating to half-grown boys at their family Christmas party many years ago in Wales.

With these four examples we have traced a progression from group convention to individual creativity: the publishers' guidelines represented the prescriptively conventionalized text-type with virtually no scope for individual style; the conference circular was a partially conventionalized text-type offering limited scope for stylistic variation; the essay combined individualistic rhetoric with a free choice of stock phrases typical in an account of musical history, while the literary text had no element of non-linguistic constraint or convention; in the case of Dylan Thomas' *A Child's Christmas in Wales* we were concerned entirely with the phenomenon of individual style, with the creative exploitation of the norms of language.

4.3 An integrated approach confirmed

At this stage, I should like to refer back to the diagram presented under 1.4 with the prototypology of text-types and criteria for translation. Chapter 2 started from the key-word 'culture' dominant in Level C of the diagram, proceeding from the relationship between language and culture (2.1) to the relationship between the source text and the communicative function of the translation (2.2). The basic conceptions of the leading theories discussed in that chapter are recognizable in the central area of the diagram: the scope of interpretation (D(i)) refers to the hermeneutic approach, with its emphasis on the understanding of the source text; the degree of precision (D(ii)) is the criterion proposed by Hönig and Kussmaul for creating a translation which relates the source text to the communicative function of the target text (D(iii)), this also being the theoretical basis of Vermeer's *Skopostheorie* and the starting point for Holz-Mänttäri's *translatorisches Handeln*. In our approach all these important criteria have been integrated. Seeing the text primarily as a product of its culture led us on to consider the problems of language norms (D(i)), language dimensions (D(ii)) and external perspective (D(iii)). The notion of conceptual identity and invariance (D(i) and D(ii)) were related to the discussion of machine translation introducing Chapter 3, which otherwise concentrated on Level E of the diagram: here text material was presented to illustrate a method of text analysis for the translator (3.2), text production (3.3), contrastive grammatical analysis (3.4) and aspects of contrastive lexical analysis (3.5).

In this chapter, we returned to the spectrum of text-types depicted in Levels A and B of the diagram; the salient points of the theories discussed in Chapter 2, situation and function, were relativized and modified to account for literary translation and the status of the literary source text. Finally, aspects of Chapter 3 were taken up again in a discussion of the relationship between text-type and individual style as against group convention.

Notes

1. Cf. 3.2 above. Beaugrande has developed and refined his alternativity theory in Beaugrande 1987.

2. Cf. Fillmore's conception of the reading process described in 3.3.

3. This can be correlated to the concept of functional equivalence (cf. Wilss 1977) or "equivalence of effect" proposed by Beaugrande 1978.

4. Cf. Enzenbergers *Nachwort* pp.129-138.

5. This information was given by the translator to members of the special research project on literary translation in Göttingen.

6. The text goes back to a script "Memories of Christmas" broadcast in BBC Wales Children's Hour on 16.12.1945 (published in *The Listener* on 20.12.1945). Speakability (see p. 35 above and Snell-Hornby 1984) was therefore a dominant criterion from the start and may account for the marked rhythm and other sound effects in the prose (see p. 127 below). This was not however considered a basic criterion in our translation critique, as the Arche-volume aims at visual presentation (cf. p. 145 below), and there is no indication that the translation was primarily intended to be read aloud. Experience has however shown that Fried's translation is in fact as rhythmical and as "speakable" as the original.

7. Holz-Mänttäri's concept of *Botschaftsträgerprofil* (1984:128ff.) can however be correlated with style, though it is not identical with it.

8. This is understood in Leech's definition (1981:13) as "the (linguistic) study of style" as in Enkvist 1973.

9. Halliday's text functions (ideational, interpersonal, textual) can be correlated with those derived from Bühler (discussed in 1.3.2), though they are not identical with them.

10. A typical example is Milic's investigation of the style of Jonathan Swift in Milic 1967.

11. This concept also goes back to the Prague School, and is particularly associated with the work of Jan Mukarovsky; cf. Vachek 1966:99f.

12. In the sense of descriptive analysis as against formalized componential analysis (cf. 3.5.1).

13. The participants are for example the *agent* (here *he*) and the *vehicle* of the verbal action (here *eyes* and *hand*).

14. This has meanwhile been designated as *register*, a much-disputed term however which has not been used here (cf. O'Donnell and Todd 1980).

5. Translation studies — future perspectives

5.1 1987 (First Edition)

> Es ist gut pflügen, wenn der Acker gereinigt ist.
> (Luther, cit. Störig 1973:20)

"It is easy to plough when the field has been cleared". This study has been an attempt to clear the ground, in the specific, metaphorical sense in which Luther applies it in the above quotation to the problems of translation. The "stones and lumps" we had — in the Lutheran sense — to clear out of the way, were unsuitable concepts (dichotomies and box-like categories), prejudices ("translation is a matter of words") and fixed ideas (such as the fixation on equivalence and dictionary equivalents). To fill the cleared space, we presented our integrated approach encompassing all text-types from literary to technical translation and including relevant aspects from related disciplines, especially linguistics. On the basis of this approach, the study will close with a tentative prognosis for the future.

Firstly, I think there is no doubt that translation studies is a discipline of the future: in a world that is rapidly growing smaller, international communication across cultures and even between the remotest corners of the earth is gradually being taken for granted, and that includes overcoming language barriers and cultural differences. Without translation the world of today with its rapid exchange of information would be unthinkable. This is one reason why translation studies has grown so rapidly over the last thirty years. What still has to be overcome is the traditional prejudice that besets it from outside: even distinguished scholars from traditional disciplines are sometimes astonished to hear that translation is not merely a matter of words, but of texts in situations. It is the most immediate task of translation studies to break down these barriers of prejudice and establish itself as a recognized independent discipline.

This firstly requires a solid theoretical basis that can throw more light on the translation process, which for too long was dismissed as either mechanical, and hence not worthy of scholarly attention, or mysterious, and hence beyond scientific analysis. An attempt to disprove both attitudes has been made here. Secondly, translation, like any other kind of specialized activity, will have to be left to the specialists and not just any native speaker or dictionary owner who happens to be available (cf. Holz-Mänttäri 1986:371; Snell-Hornby 1986a: 9ff.). The idea that anyone is qualified to translate is all the more absurd when one considers that in theory a translator is expected to be bilingual and bicultural. These lofty standards, which in practice only a select few — even among the professional translators — can satisfy, are not merely a whim of modern theorists, but (as we saw in 1.2.2 above) have been a commonplace for centuries. The complaints we read in reviews today about the poor quality of literary translations[1] and the complaints made by translators about their low status can also be found in Dryden's Preface to Ovid's *Epistles*, which was discussed at the beginning of the study. After stating his requirement that the translator of poetry should be "a genius to that art" and "a master both of his author's language and of his own" (cit. Watson 1962:271), Dryden declares:

> ... it seems to me that the true reason why we have so few versions which are tolerable is not for the too close pursuing of the author's sense, but because there are so few who have all the talents which are requisite for translation; and that there is so little praise and so small encouragement for so considerable a part of learning. (cit. Watson 1962:273)

Perhaps the most imposing list of criteria for the future translator is that put together by Louis Paulovsky in 1949 for future students at the training institute in Vienna: Paulovsky's catalogue (1983:143f.) makes such lofty demands concerning both talent and character of the future translator that one wonders if he found any candidates at all who were worthy of such a profession.

The reality of today is of course sadly different from Paulovsky's ideal: the translation institutes are notoriously overcrowded, entrance restrictions are not possible and new students are usually unaware of the demands to be made on them. Literary translators, at least in the West, are given no training at all. Such factors are bound to have a negative influence on the quality of professional translation. If they are to be overcome — and this is my second major prognosis — the newly established discipline of translation studies must decide on optimally effective study programmes for the future members of the profession — an issue which at present, especially in Western Europe, is being hotly debated (cf. Kussmaul 1986 and Stellbrink 1984 and 1985).[2]

Thirdly, given such a solid professional basis, the standard of translation critique, which is widely considered to be arbitrary and haphazard (see Reiss 1971; also Hönig and Kussmaul 1982:120ff.), should be considerably improved. That translators and publishers do react to well-founded criticism has been demonstrated by the Diogenes Verlag in Zürich. Following the publication of a critique by Klaus-Jürgen Popp on Elisabeth Schnack's German translation of Carson McCullers' novella *The Ballad of the Sad Café* (Popp 1976), which pointed out basic errors and mistranslations, stylistic weaknesses, misleading expressions and a general distortion of the author's basic message, the improvements and corrections suggested by Popp were indeed carried out.[3] Professionally trained translation scholars and professionally trained translators could in future do much to raise and maintain standards.[4]

Translation is still the step-child of scholarship. And yet it is growing ever more vital for the world of today, to further communication and to improve cultural contacts. Like many other generalizations on translation, these remarks are nothing new: the most famous statement of the kind was made by a German translator of the early 19th century called Johann Wolfgang von Goethe in a letter to Thomas Carlyle (20.07.1827): "Denn, was man auch von der Unzulänglichkeiten des Übersetzens sagen mag, so ist und bleibt es doch eins der wichtigsten und würdigsten Geschäfte in dem allgemeinen Weltwesen."

5.2 1995 (Revised Edition)

The above "future perspectives" on Translation Studies were first written nine years ago, and I should like to close the Revised Edition with a comment on how far my prognosis has been confirmed.

As regards the development of Translation Studies as a discipline of the future, we already have a comment by Susan Bassnett and André Lefevere in the introduction to their anthology of essays *Translation, History and Culture* published in 1990: "The growth of Translation Studies as a separate discipline is a success story of the 1980s. The subject has developed in many parts of the world and is clearly destined to continue developing well into the 21st century" (1990:ix). Meanwhile this process has continued, and Translation Studies (which in our definition covers translation and interpreting) is written with capital letters, but the "separate discipline", given the large number of subjects with which it overlaps, is now viewed by some, including myself, as an "interdiscipline" (see Snell-Hornby, Pöchhacker and Kaindl 1994). The approach presented here has been largely confirmed, both in the much-quoted "cultural turn" and in the fundamentally holistic perspective. Scholars working in the various spheres of Translation Studies have come closer together, and their fields of interest have started to merge. Both the skopos theory and the theory of the polysystem have proved to be outstandingly influential, and together they have provided the impetus needed to give Translation Studies the profile it has today. The potential foreseen in Theo Hermans' "new paradigm" (1985:10) has indeed been fulfilled (my few sceptical lines on the possible "ivory tower" future of the "Manipulation" approach have been deleted from this edition), and the Low Country scholars have extended their interests well beyond literary translation. Their writings are still sometimes difficult to get hold of, and older ones are all too often out of print. A welcome exception is the collection of essays by James Holmes published posthumously in 1988, with concepts and ideas which would certainly have been taken up in this book if they had been available to me when I wrote it, and which have meanwhile proved to be of fundamental importance for the development of Translation Studies. Research work is flourishing, and some of the concepts presented in this book have been applied and extended (see Kurth (1995) on the translation of metaphor and Kaindl (1995) on opera translation, also Vermeer and Witte 1990 on the scenes-and-frames concept). And finally, among the abundant publications of the last few years are some on areas I described nine years ago as neglected (see for example Oittinen 1993 on children's literature and Schultze et al. 1990 on drama translation).

These developments are also reflected in the unprecedented boom we are now witnessing all over the world in new schools, departments and even faculties for Translation Studies and the training of translators and interpreters. Within the older schools however, at least in the German-speaking area, the problems I mentioned nine years ago remain unchanged, and the attempts made to produce new study programmes (cf. Snell-Hornby 1992) are all too often hampered by the constraints of bureaucracy and prejudice. The institutes still have problems in emancipating themselves and their curricula from the influence of the traditional language departments, and massive doubts are expressed by graduates and employers as to whether students are being properly trained for their future profession. With the present international and economic developments and the breathtaking pace of technological progress,[5] the job profile of the translator is undergoing rapid changes, demanding not only language competence but also a wide range of cultural and encyclopaedic knowledge and above all a high degree of subject area expertise. With the steadily increasing need for instant information across the language barriers, international understanding and global communication, the discipline of Translation Studies and the profession of the translator and interpreter will continue to play a crucial role, and it will depend on the ability of scholars, practitioners and teachers to do justice to this role whether Translation Studies will develop into a success story of the 21st century.

Notes

1. See Winter 1981 and Reich-Ranicki 1982 as good examples.

2. The crux of the problem, as discussed by Hönig and Kussmaul and by Stellbrink, is the emancipation of the study programmes in the translation institutes from the categories of the traditional language departments. See too Snell-Hornby 1986a:25ff. The basic differences lie in the treatment of and attitudes towards the material, much of which overlaps; contrary to popular opinion, professional translators — both in training and in practice — have to translate both from and into the foreign language, and conversely, the final examinations for University language degrees (as in Great Britain and for most *Staatsexamen* in West Germany — see Sprengel 1979) require translation proficiency both from and into L2. Exceptions are Swiss universities (*Lehramtsprüfung*), which only test translation into the language of study.

3. A comparison of the 1971 and the 1981 editions of Schnack's translation, *Die Ballade vom traurigen Café*, shows this quite clearly. Independently of Popp, Billermann (1981) pointed out the same and other weaknesses in the translation, showing that University diploma theses could be an excellent instrument for monitoring the quality of literary translations.

4. See too Popovic 1984. From this argumentation it emerges quite clearly that, while older translations are most fairly approached by the descriptive method, due to historical change in the meaning and use of language (cf. 1.2.4 above), an evaluative approach is indispensable for translation studies of today and for translations of the future.

5. As is seen in the incredible advances made in computer technology over the last few years and the effect this has had on anyone working with languages. The Niemeyer guidelines reproduced in the Appendix, Text A4, with the technical details of golfball typewriters seems like a fossil of another age, but it actually only goes back to 1985.

Appendix

Text A1

Max Niemeyer Verlag

LEXICOGRAPHICA. SERIES MAIOR

Herausgegeben von

Sture Allén, Pierre Corbin, Reinhard R. K. Hartmann, Franz Josef Hausmann, Hans-Peder Kromann, Oskar Reichmann, Ladislav Zgusta

in Zusammenarbeit mit der Dictionary Society of North America (DSNA) und der European Association for Lexicography (EURALEX)

HINWEISE ZUR ERSTELLUNG DES REPRODUKTIONSFÄHIGEN MANUSKRIPTS

1. Technische Hinweise

1.1 Für die Buchreihe "Lexicographica. Series Maior" erwartet der Verlag eine reproduktionsfähige Vorlage (ausgenommen die Titelblätter), nach der der Druck fotomechanisch erfolgen kann. Nach Möglichkeit soll die Vorlage
5 mit einer IBM-Kugelkopfmaschine mit 12er-Schritteinteilung geschrieben werden.

1.2 Es ist ein *Plastikfarbband* oder 1x-Kohlefarbband zu verwenden.

1.3 Folgende *Kugelköpfe*, die gegebenenfalls der Verlag leihweise zur Verfügung stellt, sollen benützt werden:

10 Kopf 1:   Courier 10
Kopf 1a: Light Italic 12
            (Kursivschrift zu 1)

Kopf 2:   Courier 12
Kopf 2a: Courier 12
15   (Kursivschrift zu 2)

Für Sonderzeichen (z.B. eckige Klammern: Kopf Manifold 10 ~~6522 509)~~ stehen zahlreiche Kugelköpfe zur Verfügung, über die Prospekte in jeder Fachhandlung für Bürotechnik zu haben sind.

1.4 *Alle* Köpfe werden mit der 12er-Schritteinteilung geschrieben.

20 1.5 Steht nur eine Maschine mit 10er-Schritteinteilung zur Verfügung, entfallen die Schriften 2 und 2a. Der Unterschied wird dann lediglich durch verschiedenen Zeilenabstand (s. 2.2) markiert.

1.6 Steht keine Kugelkopfmaschine zur Verfügung, ist also eine kursive Auszeichnung nicht möglich, wird Kursiv-Druck durch Unterstreichung ersetzt.

25 1.7 *Zeilenabstand:* Aus Erfahrung wissen wir, daß es schwierig ist, über Abstände zu reden. Wir schlagen daher vor, die Einheit *Tuck* zu benutzen.

D-7400 Tübingen Pfrondorfer Straße 4 Postfach 2140 Telefon (07071) '8 11 04
Konten: Deutsche Bank AG Tübingen (BLZ 640 700 85) 15/03 887 Postscheckamt Stuttgart (BLZ 600 100 70) 71314-'

-2-

1 Tuck bedeutet: eine Drehung am Zeilenstellerrad. In engzeilig geschriebenen Texten ist demzufolge eine Zeile von der nächsten durch zwei Tuck entfernt, bei 1 1/2-zeilig geschriebenen Texten 3 Tuck.

2. Hinweise zur äußeren Form

2.1 Der Verlag stellt ein zum Schreiben der Reproduktionsvorlage besonders
geeignetes *Papier* (Satzspiegelvordrucke), auf dem zur Seiteneinteilung dien-
liche Hilfslinien eingedruckt sind, zur Verfügung. Die Hilfslinien werden bei
der Reproduktion unterdrückt. Alle nötigen Angaben sind auf dem beigefüg-
35   ten Musterblatt vermerkt.

2.2 Die *Köpfe* 1 und 1a werden zum Schreiben des allgemeinen Textes verwendet. Der Zeilenabstand wird für diesen Teil auf 1 1/2-zeilige Schaltung einge-
stellt.

Die Köpfe 2 und 2a werden verwendet für
40   eingeschobene Beispielsätze, längere Zitate, die eine syntaktische Einheit
bilden, tabellarische Aufstellungen usw.
Fußnoten
Bibliographie
Register und sonstige Anhänge.
45   Die mit den Köpfen 2 und 2a geschriebenen Teile werden engzeilig (1-zeilige
Schaltung) geschrieben.

2.3 *Rubriken*. Bei Kapiteln, die auf einer neuen Seite beginnen, steht die
Überschrift am oberen Satzspiegelrand; sie wird in Großbuchstaben (Kopf 1)
geschrieben. Der Text danach (oder einer zweite Überschrift) beginnt an
50   der vorgedruckten Marke.

Alle weiteren Überschriften werden normal geschrieben, der Stellenwert geht
aus der gliedernden Zählung hervor.

Über Zwischenrubriken wird der Zeilenabstand um vier Tuck (s. 1.7), danach
um zwei Tuck vergrößert.

55   Alle Überschriften stehen linksbündig (s. Muster des Satzspiegelvordrucks).

Eine neue Seite darf nie mit einer unvollständigen Zeile beginnen ("Hurenkind").
In solchen Fällen kann der Satzspiegel der vorhergehenden Seite um 1-2 Zeilen
überschritten werden.

2.4 *Anmerkungen* werden kapitelweise durchgezählt.
60   Die Hinweisziffern im Text werden hochgestellt (ohne Klammern); sie stehen
nach den Satzzeichen.

Anmerkungen stehen am Fuß der Seiten durch eine dünne Linie vom Text ge-
trennt. Die Fußnoten beginnen mit der 1. Hilfslinie nach dem linken Satzspiegelrand; davor, mit dem Satzspiegelrand bündig, steht die Zählung. Hier wird
65   die Ziffer nicht mehr hochgestellt.

2.5 *Einschaltungen* im Text (vgl. 2.2) werden gegen den vorhergehenden und
nachfolgenden Grundtext durch einen Abstand von insgesamt 4 Tuck abgesetzt.

2.6 Die *Seitenzählung* steht über dem oberen Satzspiegelrand in der vorgedruckten Markierung. Ungerade Zahlen stehen rechts außen, gerade Zahlen links
70   außen.

Einleitende Teile (Inhaltsverzeichnis, Vorwort, Abkürzungsverzeichnis usw.)
werden mit römischen Ziffern gezählt, wobei folgende Seiten, die vom Verlag
gesetzt werden, zu berücksichtigen sind: I = Reihentitel, II = Leerseite, III =
Haupttitelblatt, IV = Impressum.

Der Hauptteil wird mit arabischen Ziffern paginiert.

A2   D.R.C. Seminar on the History of Lexicography
Guidelines for presenting papers (use only space inside frame)

A.N. Author

TITLE (BLOCK CAPITALS, UNDERLINED)

The text should be typed, using 72 characters at 12 pitch, single spacing (double between paragraphs), maximum 50 lines per page, maximum 10 pages per paper. Do not number pages. (Word-processors note: no right-justification)

Footnotes should be avoided. Refer to publications by the author-date method (e.g. Collison 1982); refer to dictionaries by putting the title in capitals (e.g. CONCISE OXFORD DICTIONARY); put all bibliographical references at the end of the paper, in alpha-betical order of authors. If the paper divides into sections, use unnumbered, underlined sub-headings, as follows:

Sub-heading

A number of recent references to the literature on the history of lexicography are given below, to exemplify the preferred citation style.

References

Bahr, J. (1984) "Eine Jahrhundertleistung historischer Lexiko-graphie: Das Deutsche Wörterbuch, begründet von J. und W. Grimm" in Sprachgeschichte. Ein Handbuch zur Geschichte der deutschen Sprache und ihrer Erforschung ed. by W. Besch et al. Berlin: W. de Gruyter Vol. 1: 492-501
Collison, R.L. (1982) A History of Foreign-Language Dictionaries (The Language Library). London: Deutsch
Hausmann, F.J. and Cop, M. (1985) "Short history of English-German lexicography" in Symposium on Lexicography II ed. by K. Hyld-gaard-Jensen and A. Zettersten (Lexicographica. Series Maior 5). Tübingen: Niemeyer 183-197
Hayashi, T. (1978) The Theory of English Lexicography 1530-1791 (Amsterdam Studies in the Theory and History of Linguistic Science III.18). Amsterdam: J. Benjamins
Haywood, J.A. (1960) Arabic Lexicography: Its History and Its Place in the General History of Lexicography. Leiden: Brill
Wooldridge, T.R. (1977) Les debuts de la lexicographie française: Estienne, Nicot et le Thresor de la langue française (1606). Toronto: U.P.
Xue, S. (1982) "Chinese lexicography, past and present" Dictionaries 4: 151-169

LSA STYLE SHEET
A3 FOR PUBLICATIONS OF THE LINGUISTIC SOCIETY OF AMERICA

1. **The manuscript.** (a) Use heavy-weight paper of good quality; a 20-pound stock is best. Avoid paper that is not perfectly adapted for taking notations in ink; above all avoid Eaton's 'Corrasable Bond' and similar brands with a surface glazed for easy erasing. Xerox copies are acceptable; but avoid duplicating processes that use a glazed paper. Do not submit mimeographed or dittoed copies.

(b) Use paper of standard size, 8½ by 11 inches. If that size is not available, include a dozen extra sheets of the size you are using, for editorial purposes.

(c) All copy must be typewritten, on one side of the sheet only, double-spaced throughout. The requirement of double spacing applies to everything in the manuscript: there must not be two lines anywhere with less than a double space between. Note that 'double space' means that there is a FULL space between lines. Be warned that, on many typewriters, the second setting of the line space lever results in 'space-and-a-half,' not double space.

(d) Leave wide margins on all four sides, not less than 1½ inches at the left, the right, the top, and the bottom.

(e) Never type special matter on the same sheet with ordinary text. Special matter here denotes extended quotations and other passages to be set in smaller type, tables, charts, and diagrams, but not simple examples, rules, or formulae. Each piece of special matter must be typed (with double spacing) on a separate sheet or series of sheets. If the ordinary text preceding a piece of special matter ends with part of the sheet unfilled, leave it blank.

(f) Number the pages of the copy in the upper right corner. Include all sheets of the manuscript in a single pagination.

(g) Submit MSS of articles in three copies, of reviews in two copies. Articles will not be returned unless postage is provided by contributors. Keep a duplicate copy for yourself. (When galley proof is sent to you, the original manuscript will not be included.)

2. **Corrections.** (a) Make all the corrections of the copy as neatly and unobtrusively as possible. Avoid delete signs and other marks properly used only in correcting proof. Do not deface the copy by guide lines, rings around insertions, or instructions to the printer. Leave these to the Editor's discretion.

(b) An error discovered while typing is better corrected by x-ing out than by erasing. An error discovered later should be corrected with a fine pen (not a ball-point).

(c) To delete a single letter, x it out or draw a short vertical stroke through it. To delete a longer sequence, x it out or draw a single horizontal line through it.

(d) To insert a letter or longer sequence, write it between the lines above the point where it belongs. An addition of several words is best written in the margin, with a caret to show its place in the line. Do not draw guide lines from the addition to the caret.

(e) Never touch up a page of the manuscript with white paint, or use cellolose tape, or otherwise make it difficult for the Editor to insert pen-and-ink notations.

(f) If a page becomes hard to read because of corrections and additions, retype it. Do not paste together parts of sheets to make new sheets of abnormal size; instead, use two or more sheets of normal size, even if none is filled.

3. **Underscores.** (a) A single straight underscore indicates *italic type*, a double underscore SMALL CAPITALS, a wavy underscore boldface. Contributors are asked to use these underscorings only for the following purposes and no others.

(b) Use italics only for cited linguistic forms and for titles of books and journals. Do not use italics for emphasis, or to mark foreign words used as part of an English sentence: a-priori, ad hoc, inter alia, ipso facto, prima facie; façon de parler, langue/parole; Sprachgefühl, ursprachlich, etc.—all without underscore.

(c) Use small capitals, where it seems essential, to give prominence or emphasis to a word, phrase, or sentence in the text, or to mark a technical term at its first occurrence.

(d) Use boldface for certain forms in Oscan and Umbrian, and when necessary to distinguish Gaulish and other forms originally written in the Greek alphabet.

(e) All these type faces are occasionally used elsewhere, as in subtitles and section headings. Nevertheless, contributors should use no underscores of any kind in such headings, but should leave their choice to the Editor.

4. **Punctuation.** (a) Use only single quotation marks—never double except for quotes within quotes. This applies to all uses of quotation marks without exception. If the second of a pair of quotes stands at the same point as another mark of punctuation, the quote precedes unless the other mark is itself part of the quoted matter: The word means 'cart', not 'horse'. He writes, 'This is false.' Does that mean 'You heard me'? It means 'Did you hear me?'

(b) Never use quotes to enclose a word or

A4 LEXICOGRAPHICA. SERIES MAIOR

Edited by

Sture Allén, Pierre Corbin, Reinhard R.K. Hartmann, Franz
Josef Hausmann, Hans-Peder Kromann, Oskar Reichmann, Ladislav
Zgusta

in conjunction with the Dictionary Society of North America
(DSNA) and the European Association for Lexicography (EURALEX)

GUIDELINES FOR PRESENTING THE MANUSCRIPT

For the series "Lexicographica. Series Maior" the publishers
require camera-ready copy (except for the title pages). If
possible use an IBM golfball typewriter with characters at
12 pitch.

5   The manuscript should be typed with a plastic ribbon (or
a disposable carbon ribbon to be used once only).

Ideally Courier and Light Italic types should be used. The
following golfballs may be borrowed from the publisher:

```
        1.   Courier 10                    }
10      1a.  Light Italic 12               }  for the main text

        2.   Courier 12                    }
        2a.  Courier 12 Italic             }  for quotations, footnotes etc.
```

Where only a typewriter with characters at 10 pitch is available,
2 and 2a cannot be used, and the difference is indicated by
15 spacing, as described below.

Where there is no golfball typewriter available and italic
print is not possible, italics should be indicated by under-
scoring.

Information on golfballs with special characters (such as
20 square brackets and German ß) is available in specialist shops.

The Manuscript

The publishers provide special manuscript paper with
margins indicated by blue lines which do not appear on the
printed page (see enclosed specimen).

The main text should be typed with 1 1/2 spacing (the notch
25 between single and double spacing). Single spacing is used for:

        extended quotations and examples,
        diagrams, charts, tables,
        footnotes, bibliography and index.

Titles and headings Main chapters always start on a new
page. Type the headings in capitals (Courier 10) immediately
below the upper line of the blue frame. The text itself (or
a sub-heading) starts at the point indicated on the specimen page.

All other sub-headings are typed in normal characters
(i.e. not in capitals) and are numbered through the
chapter (e.g. 2.1., 2.2. etc.).

Before starting a new section leave two double spaces:
between a sub-heading and the following text leave a double,
and then a single space.

Start all headings at the left margin, as indicated on
the specimen page.

Never start a new page with an incomplete line ("widow").
Where necessary, rather complete the paragraph on the previous
page and continue the text below the blue frame.

Footnotes are numbered serially through the chapter. In
the text the reference number is raised (but is not enclosed
in parentheses) and is typed **after** punctuation marks.

Footnotes are placed at the bottom of the page, separated
from the text by a thin line. The reference number is typed
inside the left margin (here **not** raised), and the text of the
footnote starts at the dotted line (see specimen page).

Extended quotations, examples, diagrams etc. are separated
from the preceding and following text by a double space.

Type **page numbers** above the blue line as indicated on the
specimen (even numbers on the left, uneven numbers on the
right).

Use Roman numerals for introductory items (Table of Contents,
Preface, List of Abbreviations, etc.); allowing for the following
pages, which are provided by the publishers: I = title of series,
II = empty page, III = title page, IV = imprint.

Use Arabic numbers for the main text.

If **corrections** are necessary (words, lines, or whole paragraphs), they should be typed on the same type of paper as the
manuscript (another kind of paper would show up on the printed
page), and then pasted over the original text; use only good-
quality, heat-resistant glue.

It is also permissible to use the self-correcting unit in
a typewriter, but white paint should be avoided.

Illustrations (diagrams, tables etc.) should be presented
on good-quality drawing paper and then pasted on the manuscript.
It is also possible to use waxed tissue paper (including graph
paper with **blue** lines which are then suppressed in printing).
If any text is necessary for the illustration, do not type it
on to the waxed paper (which is unsuitable for typing), but
use the paper provided by the publisher and paste it on.

30

35

40

45

50

55

60

65

70

Text B1

PD Mary Snell-Hornby
Dekanat der Philosophischen
Fakultät I (EURALEX-Kongress)
Universität Zürich
Rämistrasse 71
CH-8006 Zürich

EUROPEAN ASSOCIATION FOR LEXICOGRAPHY

Second Circular (E/G)   20 March 1986

EURALEX International Congress

University of Zurich

9 - 14 September 1986

Preparations are now well advanced for the EURALEX International
Congress (first announced as the EURALEX Second International
Conference), which will take place at the University of Zurich
under the patronage of the Faculty of Arts. This circular is
sent to all EURALEX members and to those who have expressed
interest in the Congress. It tells you more about the Congress
itself and how to participate.

Programme

The provisional Congress programme is enclosed.

The lecture programme will be presented within a
structured framework of symposia, themes and project
reports. Individual slots vary between 45 and 30
minutes; ample time will be allowed for discussion.

A brief summary of all papers and projects to be
presented at the Congress will be included in the
Third Circular, which will be sent in July/August
to all registered, paid-up participants.

**Other
activities**

There will be plenty of opportunity for informal
contacts and discussion. On Tuesday evening a buffet
supper will be held in the University Lichthof to
help people settle in and get acquainted. On Friday
afternoon there will be an excursion on Lake Zurich
to the ancient town of Rapperswil. The other evenings
are free.

A fixed programme for guests is not envisaged, but
a guide from the Zurich Tourist Association will be
present in the Congress Office to advise on outings
and places of special interest.

An exhibition of books, dictionaries and related
projects will be mounted during the course of the
Congress.

Cost

The fee for participants, payable before 31 May 1986,
is SFr. 225 (SFr. 200 for EURALEX members). For
participants registering after 31 May 1986 there will
be a surcharge of SFr. 25. The fee includes regis-

tration, the lecture programme, the buffet supper on
Tuesday, lunch from Wednesday to Saturday inclusive,
and the excursion on Friday, but not accommodation.
Guests will be welcome at the buffet supper, the excursion, and for lunch during the Congress on payment of
a global fee of SFr. 95. Fees for participants and
guests should be paid by bank transfer as follows:

Payable to: Europäische Gesellschaft für Lexikographie
Account No.: 321.981.02 C
At: Union Bank of Switzerland (UBS)
              Bahnhofstrasse 45
              CH-8021 Zürich

Remember to give your full name and address as sender.

Note: Please pay by direct bank transfer as indicated
above, and not by sending a cheque to the organizer.

Your registration will be complete when the fee has
been received by the bank and when you have notified
the Congress Organizer of your name, institution and
full address for correspondence.

Please note that the full fee is refundable until
30 June 1986, thereafter the booking fee of SFr. 30 will
be retained. No reductions are possible for participants
who do not stay for the whole period of the Congress.

Participants who have not already done so are advised
to book their accommodation as soon as possible, as
Zurich hotels are always busy in the summer months.

**Accommo-
dation**

All bookings are being made by the Zurich Tourist
Association, to whom the enclosed booking card should
be returned by 31 July 1986 at the very latest. Please
mark clearly the required room category as specified on
the card, but do not name any particular hotel. The
Tourist Association will then book you a room of the
desired category according to what is still available.

Transport Air: World-wide connections to Zurich's International
Airport at Kloten. The Official Carrier of the EURALEX
International Congress is Swissair. Please contact your
nearest representative for any advice you may need.

Please note fare reductions for ABC bookings and for
groups of at least six persons.

Road: Zurich is situated at a central point of Switzerland's highway network and is easily accessible for long-
distance traffic. The city itself is however notoriously
difficult to negotiate for drivers who are unfamiliar
with it, and parking space near the University is limited.
Public transport is excellent in Switzerland, and participants from outside are recommended to make use of it.

Rail: Zurich is a main junction for international trains
from all neighbouring countries. Inter-City trains
usually run every hour - and they have a well-deserved
reputation for being amazingly punctual. We have made
enquiries about special rates for participants travelling
from or through Germany, and will let you have details
with the Third Circular.

B2

PD Mary Snell-Hornby
Dekanat der Philosophischen Fakultät I
[EURALEX-Kongress]
Universität Zürich
Rämistrasse 71
CH-8006 Zürich   Zürich, 20.3.1986

Zweites Rundschreiben (E/D)

Internationaler Kongress der EURALEX

Universität Zürich

9. - 14. September 1986

5 Die Vorbereitungen für den internationalen Kongress der
EURALEX (zunächst angekündigt als 2. Internationale Tagung
der EURALEX) sind bereits weit fortgeschritten. Der Kongress
findet an der Universität Zürich unter dem wissenschaftlichen
Patronat der Philosophischen Fakultät I statt. Dieses Rundschreiben wird allen EURALEX-Mitgliedern und sonstigen
Interessenten zugesandt.

Programm

10 Das vorläufige Kongressprogramm liegt bei.
Das wissenschaftliche Programm ist gegliedert in
Symposien mit anschließenden Fachreferaten und
Projektberichten. Für die einzelnen Referenten
stehen insgesamt 45 bzw. 30 Minuten zur Verfügung,
15 wobei ausreichend Zeit für Diskussionen einkalku-
liert wurde.

Eine kurze Zusammenfassung sämtlicher Referate
und Projektberichte wird im 3. Rundschreiben
enthalten sein, das im Juli/August allen ange-
meldeten Teilnehmern zugesandt wird.

Rahmen-
programm

20 Neben dem wissenschaftlichen Programm wird
ausreichend Gelegenheit für persönliche Kontakte
und Diskussionen geboten. Zum besseren gegen-
seitigen Kennenlernen findet am Dienstagabend
ein kaltes Buffet im Lichthof der Universität
25 statt. Für Freitagnachmittag ist ein Schiffs-
ausflug auf dem Zürichsee nach Rapperswil vorge-
sehen. Die übrigen Abende stehen zur freien
Verfügung.

Ein Programm für Begleitpersonen ist nicht vor-
30 gesehen, aber ein Mitarbeiter des Verkehrsvereins
Zürich wird im Kongressbüro mit Informationen über
Sehenswürdigkeiten und weitere Ausflugsmöglich-
keiten zur Verfügung stehen.

35 Im Rahmen des Kongresses wird eine Ausstellung von
Wörterbüchern und einschlägigen wissenschaftlichen
Publikationen stattfinden.

Gebühren

40 Die Teilnehmergebühr beträgt SFr. 225.-- (SFr. 200.--
für EURALEX-Mitglieder); inbegriffen sind neben der
Anmeldung und der Teilnahme am wissenschaftlichen
Programm auch das kalte Buffet am Dienstagabend, die
Mittagessen von Mittwoch bis Samstag und der Schiffs-
ausflug am Freitag, nicht jedoch die Übernachtung.
Letzter Einzahlungstermin ist der 31. Mai 1986; für
spätere Anmeldungen ist eine Zusatzgebühr von SFr. 25.--
zu entrichten. Gäste können gegen eine Pauschalgebühr
von SFr. 95.-- am kalten Buffet, an der Exkursion und
an den Mittagessen während des Kongresses teilnehmen.

45 Die Einzahlung der Gebühren für Teilnehmer und Begleit-
personen erfolgt per Überweisung auf das Konto der
Europäischen Gesellschaft für Lexikographie bei der
Schweizerischen Bankgesellschaft (SBG), Bahnhofstr. 45,
CH-8021 Zürich, Kontonummer 321.981.02 C.

50 Sie sind als Teilnehmer angemeldet, sobald Ihre Überweisung bei der Bank eingegangen ist und die Kongressleitung genaue Angaben über Ihren Namen, Ihr Institut
und Ihre Anschrift erhalten hat.

55 Bitte beachten Sie, daß im Falle einer Absage die Gebühr
nur bis zum 30. Juni 1986 in voller Höhe zurückerstattet
werden kann; nach dem 30. Juni wird eine Bearbeitungs-
gebühr von SFr. 30.-- einbehalten. Die volle Teilnehmergebühr ist auch dann zu bezahlen, wenn Sie nicht für
die gesamte Dauer des Kongresses anwesend sind.

Unter-
kunft

60 Es empfiehlt sich, die Unterkunft möglichst rechtzeitig
zu bestellen, da die Zürcher Hotels in den Sommermonaten
meist ausgebucht sind.

65 Die Reservierung erfolgt über den Verkehrsverein Zürich,
an den die beiliegende Bestellkarte bis spätestens
31. Juli 1986 zu senden ist. Bitte kreuzen Sie die
gewünschte Zimmerkategorie an, ohne jedoch ein bestimmtes
Hotel zu nennen. Der Verkehrsverein Zürich wird Ihnen ein
Zimmer der gewünschten Kategorie je nach Verfügbarkeit
besorgen.

Anreise

70 Flugverbindungen: Zürich/Kloten wird aus aller Welt
angeflogen mit direkten Verbindungen aus den meisten
europäischen Ländern. Die offizielle Fluggesellschaft
des EURALEX-Kongresses ist Swissair.

75 Beachten Sie die Preisermäßigungen für Apex-Buchungen
und für Gruppen von mindestens 6 Personen!

Straßenverbindungen: Zürich ist von der Autobahn her
bequem zu erreichen. In der Stadt selbst jedoch ist der
"Verkehrssalat" berüchtigt, und die Parkmöglichkeiten in
80 der Nähe der Universität sind sehr begrenzt. Es wird
empfohlen, die ausgezeichneten öffentlichen Verkehrs-
mittel in Anspruch zu nehmen.

85 Bahnverbindungen: Zürich ist ein Hauptknotenpunkt im
internationalen Zugverkehr. Inter-City-Züge fahren
meist im Stundentakt. Die Kongressleitung bemüht sich
um eine Preisermäßigung für Teilnehmer, die von oder
durch Deutschland anreisen; nähere Einzelheiten
erfahren Sie im 3. Rundschreiben.

Text C1

Dr. Thea Lethmair

Eine Stadt
mit erstaunlichen
Dirigentenwundern

Augsburg, die „Opernstadt", in der Wagners „Ring" seit der Jahrhundertwende „Pflicht" ist, in der der Intendant Dr. Karl Bauer im Lauf einer Diskussionsrunde einmal von einer opernbesessenen Bäckermeisterin ungeduldig ge-
5 fragt wurde, „Ja, wann kommt den jetzt endlich „Die Götterdämmerung"? — Augsburg, wo Spitzenwerke des Repertoires, als da sind „Meistersinger", „Parsifal", „Rosenkavalier" noch bis in die sechziger Jahre mit hauseigenen Kräften in Doppelbesetzung einstudiert werden konnten
10 und große Meister zyklisch aufgeführt werden — wie käme sie zu solchem Ansehen ohne seine Dirigenten? Seit einige von ihnen unvorhersehbares Format gezeigt haben, spricht man von Augsburg auch als der Stadt des „Dirigentenwunders". Wunder entziehen sich rationalem Bemü-
15 hen. Da das Theater sich auf alle Fälle darum bemühen muß, seine musikalischen Pflichtaufgaben (möglichst gut) zu bewältigen, kann es sich nicht allein auf Wunder verlassen. Folglich gibt es in der Augsburger Operngeschichte seit den frühen Anfängen dieses Jahrhunderts Dirigenten
20 mit und ohne Wunder, wobei jene ohne Wunder an Verdiensten nicht minder reich sind.

Ohne Wunder im späteren Sinn, als dieser Begriff nicht unwesentlich mit dem Prestissimo einer Karriere zusammenhängt, aber von höchst imponierendem Können, war
25 Josef Bach, der erste Städtische Kapellmeister des Theaters nach dem 1. Weltkrieg, zwölf Jahre im Amt (1919—1931). Damals begnügt man sich noch mit bescheidenen Titulaturen. Die außerordentliche technische Versiertheit, die ihn befähigt, Musikern (damals etwa 45 Mann) ein anspruchs-
30 volles, breit gestreutes Repertoire abzuverlangen, bringt ihn in die Gefahr als „Routinier" zu gelten. Er ist es im besten Sinne, in jenem des umfassenden Könners. Als Musiker „von gesundem und zugleich kultiviertem Instinkt", als hervorragender Orchestererzieher, „legt er den Grund,
35 auf dem die späteren städtischen Kapellmeister . . . weiterbauen" können. So Willi Leininger in der Festschrift zum 100jährigen Bestehen des Orchesters 1965.

Der zweite Kapellmeister jener Jahre, Karl Tutein (1918—1928), sein Talent am Pult u.a. bei Pfitzner („Der
40 arme Heinrich"), Janacek („Jenufa") und Strauss („Salome" und „Elektra") erweisend, wechselt vom Lech unmittelbar zur Münchner Staatsoper. Josef Bach wird anschließend an seine Theaterarbeit in Augsburg Konservatoriumsdirektor, ein Terrainwechsel, den noch einige
45 Kollegen nach ihm vollziehen. Ein Pionier der Moderne

322

ist Ewald Lindemann (1931—1933), Typ des intellektuellen Musikers mit besonderer Vorliebe für Strawinsky.

Musikalische Statthalter

Martin Engelkraut (1933—1945) steht die zwölf Jahre des „Tausendjährigen Reichs" an der Spitze des Orchesters. Aus Chemnitz bringt er nicht nur souveräne Beherr- 50 schung des Repertoires und der Orchesterpraxis sondern auch den Titel „Operndirektor" mit, den er als erster am neuen Wirkungsort trägt. Aus Bayreuth zudem ausgedehnte Wagner-Praxis, gewonnen in mehreren Assistentenjahren. Eine Gesamtaufführung des „Ring der Nibelungen" 55 präsentiert er gleich im ersten Amtsjahr. Egelkraut, Typus des grundsoliden, der Tradition verhafteten deutschen Kapellmeisters, widmet sich daneben ausgiebiger Strauss-Pflege. In seiner Aegide erfährt neben „Arabella" und „Friedenstag" auch die sehr anspruchsvolle „Daphne" eine 60 bedeutende Aufführung. Als starke Persönlichkeit profiliert sich neben Egelkraut der erste Kapellmeister Dr. Heinz Röttger, Strauss-Spezialist, bedeutender Komponist, ausgezeichneter Pianist und Kammermusik-Spieler, später Generalmusikdirektor in Dessau. 65

Arthur Piechlers Verdienste

Die ersten Dirigenten in der Zeit zwischen den beiden Weltkriegen verkörpern den Typus des musikalischen Statthalters. Augsburg hat für sie den Stellenwert einer Endstation, zumindest einer Station, in die sie volle Metier-Beherrschung und Praxis-Erfahrung mitbringen. 70 Reiselust ist ihnen so fremd wie der Begriff „Chefdirigent", der noch nicht offfiziell auftaucht. Was sich nach 1945, wie so vieles, ändert. Erste Bedingung ist damals: „unbelastete" Musiker zum Wiederaufbau des Orchesters und einen „unbelasteten" Dirigenten zu finden. Beides ge- 75 lingt Prof. Arthur Piechler, der sich das ewige Verdienst des Wiederaufbaus der Augsburger Musikkultur erwirbt. Mit Fritz Schnell gewinnt er dem Orchester einen feinnervigen, künstlerisch integren Dirigenten mit der nötigen Anstrengungsbereitschaft, die die Aufbauarbeit in den er- 80 sten Nachkriegsjahren mit dem improvisierten Spielbetrieb im Ludwigsbau erfordert. Nur ein Jahr bleibt Fritz Schnell tritt an seine Seite Kapellmeister Anton Mooser (1946—1976), geflüchtet aus Königsberg.

C2

Keeping up Tradition: A City of Great Maestros

Augsburg is a city with a well-established operatic tradition. Wagner's "Ring" has been part of the repertoire since the turn of the century — much to the delight of the opera-loving citizens — and right up into the sixties great 5 works such as "The Mastersingers", "Parsifal" and "Der Rosenkavalier" were regularly produced with both cast and understudies contracted to the house — and how would all this have been possible without first-rate conductors? As some of them have even shown an unforeseen 10 brilliance, Augsburg has been given the title "City of Great Maestros".

A man of imposing expertise was Josef Bach, the first Kapellmeister at the City Theatre after the First World War. He held this post for twelve years (1919—1931). His 15 exceptional technical abilities, which enabled him to demand from his 45 musicians a broad and difficult repertoire, may have earned him the image of a "well-trained man of routine" — in fact he is better described as an all-round expert. As a musician "with sound and cultivated 20 instincts", and as an outstanding orchestral leader, "he laid the foundations upon which later conductors could build". Those are the words of Willi Leininger in the book published to celebrate the orchestra's centenary in 1965.

Bach's deputy of those years, Karl Tutein (1918—1928), 25 after showing his talent in works by Pfitzner, Janacek and Richard Strauss, went from Augsburg straight on to a post at the Munich State Opera. After his work for the theatre, Josef Bach was appointed director of the Augsburg Conservatory of Music, a move that was later to be copied by 30 some of his colleagues. His successor, Ewald Lindemann (1931—1933), was a pioneer of modern music, an intellectual with a preference for Stravinsky.

Martin Egelkraut (1933—1945) led the orchestra for the twelve years of the "Thousand-year Reich". From Chem- 35 nitz he brought not only orchestral experience and superb mastery of a broad repertoire, but also the title of "Operatic Director", which he was the first to bear in Augsburg. In Bayreuth he had gained experience with Wagner's works while serving as assistant for many years. So it was 40 only natural that in this first year he produced the full "Ring of the Nibelungen". Sound and reliable, and of traditional leanings, he also devoted special attention to Richard Strauss. Under his baton there were some significant performances of "Arabella" and "Friedenstag" and 45 the extremely difficult work "Daphne". His chief conduc-

268

tor, Dr. Heinz Röttger, was himself a Strauss specialist, as well as a composer of repute, an excellent pianist and chamber musician, and later on he became General Director of Music at Dessau.

Arthur Piechler's Achievement

For the conductors between the wars, Augsburg was a 50 place to settle after gaining experience and a command of their metier. The desire to travel was foreign to them as was the title "Chefdirigent" or "First Conductor", which had not yet been officially introduced. After 1945 this, like so much else, all changed. In those days the main thing 55 was to find both musicians and a conductor who were untarnished by a Nazi past. Professor Arthur Piechler succeeded in doing just that. In Fritz Schnell he found a sensitive yet unaffected conductor who was prepared to undertake the demanding task of reshaping the orchestra in the post- 60 war years, playing under improvised conditions in the Ludwig concert hall.

Anton Mooser's Records

A year later Fritz Schnell was joined by Anton Mooser (1946—1976), a spirited Bavarian musician from Freilassing, who was to become the record-holder of the City Theatre. 65 He worked there vor 30 years, first as Kapellmeister and then as Schnell's successor in the post of General Director of Music. During this time he conducted 1739 performances, of these 152 were premières. He had an unusually varied repertoire centred round Mozart, Wagner, Verdi 70 and Strauss. With Hannes Schönfelder and the set designer Hans Ulrich Schmückle, he created the first "Ring" in the new Bayreuth style. In 1956, at the opening of the rebuilt theatre, he conducted "The Marriage of Figaro" in best Mozart tradition. After his work at the theatre Anton 75 Mooser, like Fritz Schnell, became Director of the Leopold Mozart Conservatory in Augsburg.

Sawallisch, the All-round Genius

In 1947 a young choirmaster came straight from th Munich College of Music to the theatre at Augsburg: hi

Text D

One Christmas was so much like another, in
those years, around the sea-town corner now,
and out of all sound except the distant speaking
of the voices I sometimes hear a moment before
5 sleep, that I can never remember whether it
snowed for six days and six nights when I was
twelve or whether it snowed for twelve days
and twelve nights when I was six; or whether
the ice broke and the skating grocer vanished
10 like a snowman through a white trap-door on
that same Christmas Day that the mince-pies
finished Uncle Arnold and we tobogganed down
the seaward hill, all the afternoon, on the best
tea-tray, and Mrs Griffiths complained, and we
15 threw a snowball at her niece, and my hands
burned so, with the heat and the cold, when
I held them in front of the fire, that I cried for
twenty minutes and then had some jelly.

All the Christmases roll down the hill towards
the Welsh-speaking sea, like a snowball growing
20 whiter and bigger and rounder, like a cold and
headlong moon bundling down the sky that was
our street; and they stop at the rim of the

Ein Weihnachten war so sehr wie das andere
in jenen Jahren, die nun um die Meerecke der
Stadt entschwunden und außer aller Hörweite
sind, bis auf das ferne Gespräch ihrer Stimmen,
5 die ich manchmal einen Augenblick lang vor dem
Einschlafen hören kann, daß ich jetzt nie mehr
sagen kann, ob es sechs Tage und sechs Nächte
lang geschneit hat, als ich zwölf war, oder ob es
zwölf Tage und zwölf Nächte lang geschneit hat,
10 als ich sechs war. Oder damals, als das Eis brach
und der Schlittschuh laufende Schnittwaren-
händler verschwand wie ein Schneemann durch
eine weiße Falltür, ob das derselbe Weihnachtstag
war, an dem die Rosinenkuchen Onkel Arnold
15 halb krank machten und wir den seeseitigen
Hügel hinunterrodelten, den ganzen Nachmittag
lang, auf dem besten Teetablett; und
Mrs. Griffith beschwerte sich, und wir warfen
einen Schneeball nach ihrer Nichte, und als ich
20 die Hände vors Feuer hielt, da brannten sie vor
Kälte und Hitze so sehr, daß ich zwanzig Minuten
lang weinte; und dann aß ich Wackelpudding.

Alle Weihnachten rollen den Hügel hinunter zum
walisisch sprechenden Meer, wie ein Schneeball,
25 der immer weißer und größer und runder
wird, wie ein kalter und kopfüber kollernder
Mond, der den Himmel hinunterkollert, der un-

ice-edged, fish-freezing waves, and I plunge
my hands in the snow and bring out whatever I
can find; holly or robins or pudding, squabbles
and carols and oranges and tin whistles, and the
fire in the front room, and bang go the crackers,
and holy, holy, holy, ring the bells, and the glass
bells shaking on the tree, and Mother Goose,
and Struwelpeter – oh! the baby-burning flames
and the clacking scissorman! – Billy Bunter and
Black Beauty, Little Women and boys who have
three helpings, Alice and Mrs.Potter's badgers,
penknives, teddy-bears – named after a Mr.
Theodore Bear, their inventor, or father, who
died recently in the United States – mouth-organs
tin-soldiers, and blancmange, and Auntie Bessie
playing 'Pop Goes the Weasel' and 'Nuts in
May' and 'Oranges and Lemons' on the untuned
piano in the parlour all through the thimble-
hiding musical-chairing blind-man's-buffing
party at the end of the never-to-be-forgotten day
at the end of the unremembered year.

sere Straße war; und alle Weihnachten machen
halt am Ufer der eisgeränderten, fische-frierenden Wellen, und ich fahre mit den Händen tief
in den Schnee und hole alles heraus, was ich
finden kann: Tannenzweige und Weihnachtssing-
vögel, oder Pudding, Gezänk und Choräle, und
Orangen und blecherne Pfeifchen, und das
Kaminfeuer in der guten Stube, und Bums die
Knallbonbons, und Heilig, heilig, heilig läuten
die Glocken, und die Glasglocken beben am
Baum, und Mutter Graugans aus der Weih-
nachtspantomime, und der Struwwelpeter – ach,
die paulinchen-verbrennenden Flammen und der
klappernde Scherenmann. Und Billy Bunter aus
dem bunten Groschenheft und die schwarze
Schönheit, und Goldelse und die kleine Frau;
und Jungen, die drei Portionen essen, und Alice
im Wunderland und Mrs. Potters Dachse, und
Federmesser und Teddybären – benannt nach
einem Mr. Theodor Bär, ihrem Erfinder oder
Vater, der vor kurzem in den Vereinigten
Staaten starb –, Mundharmonikas, Bleisoldaten
und Milchpudding und Tante Bessy, die auf dem
ungestimmten Piano in der guten Stube «Ein
Männlein steht im Walde» und «Orangen und
Lemonen» spielt, den ganzen Pfänder und
Blindekuh spielenden Abend lang, am Ende des
unvergeßlichen Tages, am Ende des nicht mehr
erinnerten Jahres.

List of source texts

Carroll, Lewis. 1908/1947. *Alice's Adventures in Wonderland*, London: Heinemann.
-----. 1963. *Alice im Wunderland*, übersetzt und mit einem Nachwort von Christian Enzensberger, Frankfurt: Insel.
Durrell, Lawrence. 1958. *Balthazar*, London: Faber.
-----. 1965. *Balthazar*, tr. by Gerda von Uslar and Maria Carlsson, Hamburg: Rowohlt.
Isherwood, Christopher. 1935. *Mr Norris Changes Trains*, London: Hogarth.
Mann, Thomas. 1936. "The Infant Prodigy," in: *Stories of Three Decades*, translated from the German by H.T. Lowe-Porter, New York: Modern Library, 173-180.
-----. 1958. "Das Wunderkind," in: W. Killy (ed.), *Zeichen der Zeit. Ein deutsches Lesebuch, Band 4, Verwandlung und Wirklichkeit*, Frankfurt: Fischer, 50-57.
Maugham, William Somerset. 1953. "Der Stille Ozean," in: *Betörende Südsee*, translated by Ilse Krämer, Zürich: Arche.
-----. 1961. "The Pacific," in: *The Trembling of a Leaf*, London: Heinemann.
McCullers, Carson. 1971, 1981. *Die Ballade vom traurigen Café. Novelle.* Aus dem Amerikanischen von Elisabeth Schnack, Zürich: Diogenes.
Schweinberger, W. (ed.) 1984. *2000 Jahre Augsburg. Das Buch zum Jubiläum*, Augsburg: AWO-Werbung GmbH.
-----. 1985. *Augsburg: 2000 years. The Jubilee Book*, Augsburg: AWO-Werbung GmbH.
Stoppard, Tom. 1972. *Jumpers*, London: Faber.
-----. 1976. *Akrobaten*, translated by Hilde Spiel, Hamburg: Rowohlt.
Thomas, Dylan. (n.d.). *Eines Kindes Weihnacht in Wales*. Eine Erzählung Englisch-Deutsch, translated by Erich Fried, Zürich: Arche.
Neue Zürcher Zeitung, 7.4.1978.

Süddeutsche Zeitung, 12.4.1984 and 3.10.1985.

TIME Magazine, 24.12.1984.

Die Zeit, 23.3.1984.

D.R.C. Seminar on the History of Lexicography, Exeter. Guidelines for presenting papers.

EURALEX International Congress, University of Zürich, September 1986, Second Circular (English and German).

LSA Style Sheet for publications of the Linguistic Society of America.

Max Niemeyer Verlag, Lexicographica. Series Maior. Hinweise zur Erstellung des reproduktionsfähigen Manuskripts.

Official Guide to the Castle Museum in York.

List of dictionaries

ALD – *Oxford Advanced Learner's Dictionary of Current English*, ed. A.S. Hornby, Oxford: Oxford University Press, 1974.

BW – *Brockhaus-Wahrig. Deutsches Wörterbuch* (6 vols.), ed. Gerhard Wahrig et al., Wiesbaden: Brockhaus, 1980-1985.

CED – *Collins Dictionary of the English Language*, ed. Patrick Hanks et al., London: Collins, 1979.

COD – *The Concise Oxford Dictionary of Current English*, ed. H.W. Fowler et al., Oxford: Clarendon, 1976.

Du – *Duden. Das große Wörterbuch der deutschen Sprache in sechs Bänden*, ed. Günter Drosdowski et al., Mannheim: Bibl. Institut, 1976-1981.

HC – *Harrap's Concise Dictionary* (English-German), ed. Robin Sawer, London: Harrap, 1983.

LEnz – *Langenscheidts Enzyklopädisches Wörterbuch (Deutsch/ Englisch)*, ed. H. Messinger et al., München: Langenscheidt, 1977.

OED – *The Oxford English Dictionary* (12 vols.), ed. J.A.H. Murray et al., Oxford: Clarendon, 1933.

P/C – *Pons/Collins Global-Wörterbuch Englisch/Deutsch*, (2 vols.), ed. Roland Breitsprecher et al., Stuttgart: Klett, 1983.

Wi – *Wildhagen, English-German, German-English Dictionary, Vol.1, English-German*, ed. W. Heraucourt, Wiesbaden: Brandstetter, 1973.

WdG – *Wörterbuch der deutschen Gegenwartssprache* (6 vols.), ed. W. Steinitz and R. Klappenbach, Berlin: Akademie, 1981-

Sanders, Daniel, *Wörterbuch der deutschen Sprache. Mit Belegen von Luther bis auf die Gegenwart*, Leipzig, 1860-1865, rpt. 1976.

Weber, Ferdinand Adolf, *Handwörterbuch der deutschen Sprache*. Leipzig, 1908.

Bibliography

Anttila, Raimo. 1977. "Dynamic fields and linguistic structure: A proposal for a Gestalt linguistics," in: *Sprache* 23,1-10.

Arntz, Reiner. 1986. "Terminologievergleich und internationale Terminologieangleichung," in: M. Snell-Hornby (ed.), *Übersetzungswissenschaft — Eine Neuorientierung*, 283-310.

Austin, J.L. 1962. *How to Do Things with Words*, Oxford: Clarendon.

Ayto, John. 1988. "Fig. leaves. Metaphor in dictionaries," in: M. Snell-Hornby (ed.), *ZüriLEX '86 Proceedings*, Tübingen: Francke.

Bar-Hillel, Y. 1960. "The Present Status of Automatic Translation of Languages," in: *Advances in Computers*, Vol.1, New York: Academic Press.

Barthes, Roland. 1966. *Critique et Vérité*, Paris: Editions du Seuil.

Bassnett(-McGuire), Susan. 1980 rev. 1991. *Translation Studies*, London: Methuen.

-----. 1985. "Ways Through the Labyrinth. Strategies and Methods for Translating Theatre Texts," in: T. Hermans (ed.), *The Manipulation of Literature*, 87-102.

Bassnett, Susan and André Lefevere (eds.). 1990. *Translation, History and Culture*, London: Pinter.

Bausch, Karl-Richard and Hans-Martin Gauger (eds.). 1971. *Interlinguistica. Sprachvergleich und Übersetzen. Festschrift zum 60. Geburtstag von Mario Wandruszka*, Tübingen: Niemeyer.

Bausch, Karl-Richard and Franz-Rudolf Weller (eds.). 1981. *Übersetzen und Fremdsprachenunterricht*, Frankfurt: Diesterweg.

Beaugrande, Robert de. 1978. *Factors in a Theory of Poetic Translating*, Assen: Van Gorcum.

-----. 1987. "Schemas for Literary Communication," in: L. Halász (ed.), *Literary Discourse. Aspects of Cognitive and Social Psychological Approaches*, Berlin: de Gruyter, 49-99.

-----. 1988. "Text and Process in Translation," in: R. Arntz (ed.), *Textlinguistik und Fachsprache. Akten des Internationalen übersetzungswissenschaftlichen AILA-Symposions Hildesheim, 13.-16. April 1987*, Hildesheim: Olms, 413-432.

Beaugrande, Robert de and Wolfgang Dressler. 1981. *Einführung in die Textlinguistik*, Tübingen: Niemeyer.

Berlin, Brent, Dennis E. Breedlove and Peter H. Raven. 1974. *Principles of Tzeltal Plant Classification*, New York: Academic Press.

Bierod, Sylvia. 1982. *Methoden der semantischen Analyse, dargestellt an kontrastiven Wortfelduntersuchungen im Deutschen und Englischen*, Diploma thesis, unpubl. ms., Heidelberg.

Billermann, Angelika. 1981. *Carson McCullers: "The Ballad of the Sad Café." Eine Kritik der deutschen Übersetzung "Die Ballade vom traurigen Café" von Elisabeth Schnack*, Diploma thesis, unpubl. ms., Heidelberg.

Bloomfield, Leonard. 1933. *Language*, rpt. London: Allen, 1976.

Bolinger, Dwight. 1965. "The atomization of meaning," in: *Language* 41, 555-573.

Brislin, R.W. (ed.) 1976. *Translation: Applications and Research*, New York: Gardner.

Bühler, Karl. [2]1965. *Sprachtheorie*, Stuttgart: Fischer.

Cary, Edmond. 1963. *Les grands traducteurs français*, Geneva: Univ.Press.

Catford, J.C. 1965. *A Linguistic Theory of Translation*, London: Oxford University Press.

Coseriu, Eugenio. 1970. "System, Norm und Rede," in: E. Coseriu, *Sprache, Strukturen und Funktionen*, Tübingen: Narr, 193-212.

-----. 1971. "Thesen zum Thema 'Sprache und Dichtung'," in: W.-D. Stempel (ed.), *Beiträge zur Textlinguistik*, München: Fink, 183-188.

Cowie, Anthony P. (ed.) 1987. *The Dictionary and the Language Learner. Papers from the EURALEX Seminar at the University of Leeds, 1-3 April 1985*, Tübingen: Niemeyer.

Croce, Benedetto. 1902/1955. *Filosofia, poesia, storia: Pagine tratteda tutte le opere a cara dell' autore*, 3 vols., Milano: Ricciardi.

Crystal, David and Derek Davy. 1969. *Investigating English Style*, London: Longman.

Dagut, Menachim. 1976. "Can 'Metaphor' be Translated?," in: *Babel* XII, 21-33.

Diller, Hans-Jürgen and Joachim Kornelius. 1978. *Linguistische Probleme der Übersetzung*, Tübungen: Niemeyer.

Dryden, John. 1962. *Of dramatic poesy*, ed. George Watson, London: Dent.

Enkvist, Nils E. 1973. *Linguistic Stylistics*, Den Haag: Mouton.

Even-Zohar, Itamar. 1978. *Papers in Historical Poetics*, Tel Aviv: Porter Institute.

-----. 1979. "Polysystem Theory," in: *Poetics Today* 1-2, 287-310.

Filipec, J. 1971. "Der Äquivalenzbegriff und das Problem der Übersetzbarkeit," in: *Beiheft V/VI der Zeitschrift Fremdsprachen*, 81-85.

Fillmore, Charles J. 1977. "Scenes-and-frames semantics," in: A. Zampolli (ed.), *Linguistic Structures Processing*, Amsterdam: N. Holland, 55-81.

-----. 1982. "Towards a Descriptive Framework for Spatial Deixis," in: E. Jarvella and W. Klein (eds.), *Speech, Place and Action*, London: Wiley, 31-54.

Firth, John R. 1957. *Papers in Linguistics 1934-1951*, London: Oxford University Press.

-----. 1968. *Selected Papers*, ed. Frank R. Palmer, London: Longman.

-----. 1970. *The Tongues of Men* and *Speech*, London: Oxford University Press.

Forget, Philippe. 1981. "Übersetzen als Sprachverhalten," in: *Mitteilungsblatt für Dolmetscher und Übersetzer* 4, 1-8.

Gadamer, Hans-Georg. 1960. *Wahrheit und Methode. Grundzüge einer philosophischen Hermeneutik*, Tübingen: Mohr.

Gerzymisch-Arbogast, Heidrun. 1986. "Zur Relevanz der Thema-Rhema-Gliederung für den Übersetzungsprozeß," in: M. Snell-Hornby (ed.), *Übersetzungswissenschaft — Eine Neuorientierung*, 160-183.

-----. 1987. *Zur Thema-Rhema-Gliederung in amerikanischen Wirtschaftstexten. Eine exemplarische Analyse*, Tübingen: Narr.

Godel, Robert. 1981. "La linguistique de la parole," in: H. Weydt (ed.), *Lagos semantikos. Studia linguistica in honorem Eugonio Coseriu 1921-1981*, Vol.II, Berlin: de Gruyter, 45-57.

Göhring, Heinz. 1977. "Interkulturelle Kommunikation: Die Überwindung der Trennung von Fremdsprachen- und Landeskundeunterricht durch einen integrierten Fremdverhaltensunterricht," in: *Kongreßberichte der 8. Jahrestagung der Gesellschaft für Angewandte Linguistik GAL e.V.*, Vol.IV, Mainz, 9-13.

Goodenough, Ward H. 1964. "Cultural Anthropology and Linguistics," in: D. Hymes (ed.), *Language in Culture and Society. A Reader in Linguistics and Anthropology*, New York: Harper & Row, 36-40.

Grähs, L., G. Korlén and B. Malmberg. 1978. *Theory and Practice of Translation*, Bern: Lang.

Greimas, Algirdas J. 1974. "Die Isotopie der Rede," in: W. Kallmeyer et al. (eds.), *Lektürekolleg zur Textlinguistik*, Vol.2, *Reader*, Frankfurt: Athenäum, 126-152.

Gutknecht, Christoph. 1987. "Kanada — ein 'klassisches' Land des Übersetzens? Anmerkungen zum Stand von Theorie und Praxis der Translation in einer bilingualen Nation," in: F.H. Bastein (ed.), *Kanada heute: Hamburger Beiträge zu Raum, Gesellschaft und Kultur*, Frankfurt: Lang, 225-261.

Güttinger, Fritz. 1963. *Zielsprache. Theorie und Technik des Übersetzens*, Zürich: Manesse.

Halliday, M.A.K. 1976. *System and Function in Language. Selected Papers*, ed. G.R. Kress, Cambridge: Cambridge University Press.

Halliday, M.A.K. and Ruqaia Hasan. 1976. *Cohesion in English*, London: Longman.

Hanks, Patrick. 1985. "Evidence and intuition in lexicography," in: J. Tomaszczyk (ed.), *International Conference on Meaning and Lexicography. Abstracts*, Łódź: English Institute, 22-23.

-----. 1988. "Dictionaries and meaning potentials," in: M. Snell-Hornby (ed.), *ZüriLEX '86 Proceedings*, Tübingen: Francke.

Hartmann, Reinhard R.K. 1980. *Contrastive Textology. Comparative Discourse Analysis in Applied Linguistics*, Heidelberg: Groos.

-----. 1989. "Contrastive Linguistics and Bilingual Lexicography," in: H.E. Wiegand et al. (eds.), *Handbuch der Lexikographie Bd 5.1*, Art.299.

Hellinger, Marlis. 1977. *Kontrastive Grammatik. Deutsch/Englisch*, Tübingen: Niemeyer.

Hermans, Theo (ed.) 1985. *The Manipulation of Literature. Studies in Literary Translation*, London: Croom Helm.

Hofmann, Norbert. 1980. *Redundanz und Äquivalenz in der literarischen Übersetzung, dargestellt an fünf deutschen Übersetzungen des Hamlet*, Tübingen: Niemeyer.

Holmes, James S. (ed.) 1970. *The Nature of Translation*, The Hague: Mouton.

-----. 1985. "The State of Two Arts: Literary Translation and Translation Studies in the West Today," in: H. Bühler (ed.), *X. Weltkongreß der FIT. Kongreßakte*, Wien: Braumüller, 147-153.

-----. 1988. *Translated! Papers on Literary Translation and Translation Studies*, Amsterdam: Rodopi.

Holmes, James S., José Lambert and Raymond van den Broeck. (eds.)
1978. *Literature and Translation: New Perspectives in Literary Studies*,
Leuven: Acco.

Holz-Mänttäri, Justa. 1984. *Translatorisches Handeln. Theorie und
Methode*, Helsinki: Suomalainen Tiedeakatemia.

-----. 1986. "Translatorisches Handeln — theoretisch fundierte
Berufsprofile," in: M. Snell-Hornby (ed.), *Übersetzungswissenschaft —
Eine Neuorientierung*, 348-374.

Holzheuser, Hanno. 1986. *Wörterbuch als Fehlerquelle — Ein Vergleich
lexikalischer Einträge*, Diploma thesis, unpubl. ms., Heidelberg.

Hönig, Hans G. 1986. "Übersetzen zwischen Reflex und Reflexion — ein
Modell der übersetzungsrelevanten Textanalyse," in: M. Snell-Hornby
(ed.), *Übersetzungswissenschaft — Eine Neuorientierung*, 230-251.

Hönig, Hans G. and Paul Kußmaul. 1982. *Strategie der Übersetzung. Ein
Lehr- und Arbeitsbuch*, Tübingen: Narr.

Hörmann, Hans. 1976. *Meinen und Verstehen. Grundzüge einer
psychologischen Semantik*, Frankfurt: Suhrkamp.

House, Juliane. 1977. *A Model for Translation Quality Assessment*,
Tübingen: Narr.

Humboldt, Wilhelm von. 1977. "Natur der Sprache überhaupt. 1824-1926,"
in: H.H. Christmann (ed.), *Sprachwissenschaft des 19. Jahrhunderts*,
Darmstadt: Wiss. Buchgesellschaft, 19-46.

Husserl, Edmund. 1913. *Ideen zu einer reinen Phänomenologie und
phänomenologischen Philosophie*, The Hague: Nijhoff.

Hymes, Dell. (ed.) 1964. *Language in Culture and Society: A Reader in
Linguistics and Anthropology*, New York: Harper & Row.

Iser, Wolfgang. 1976. *Der Akt des Lesens. Theorie ästhetischer Wirkung*,
München: Fink.

Jäger, Gert. 1975. *Translation und Translationslinguistik*, Halle.

Jakobson, Roman. 1959. "On Linguistic Aspects of Translation," in: R.
Brower (ed.), *On Translation*, Cambridge, Mass. 232-239.

Jerome (Saint). 1980. *Liber de optime genere interpretandi* (Epistula 57),
ed. G.J.M. Bartelink, Leiden: Brill.

Kade, Otto. 1968. *Zufall und Gesetzmäßigkeit in der Übersetzung. Beiheft
zur Zeitschrift Fremdsprachen I*, Leipzig.

Kaindl, Klaus. 1995. *Die Oper als Textgestalt. Perspektiven einer interdiszip-
linären Übersetzungswissenschaft*, Tübingen: Stauffenburg.

Kaiser-Cooke, Michèle. 1993. *Machine Translation and the Human Factor. Knowledge and Decision-making in the Translation Process.* Vienna, doctoral thesis, unpubl. ms.

Katz, Jerrold J. 1972. *Semantic Theory*, Cambridge: Cambridge University Press.

Kelly, L.G. 1979. *The True Interpreter. A History of Translation Theory and Practice in the West*, Oxford: Blackwell.

Klein-Braley, Christine. 1982. "Die Übersetzung als Testverfahren in der Staatsprüfung für Lehramtskandidaten," in: *Neusprachliche Mitteilungen* 2, 94-97.

Kloepfer, Rolf. 1967. *Die Theorie der literarischen Übersetzung. Romanisch-deutscher Sprachbereich*, München: Fink.

Koller, Werner. 1972. *Grundprobleme der Übersetzungstheorie. Unter besonderer Berücksichtigung schwedisch-deutscher Übersetzungsfälle*, Bern: Francke.

-----. 1979. *Einführung in die Übersetzungswissenschaft*, Heidelberg: Quelle & Meyer.

Kornelius, Joachim. 1982. "Übersetzungsübungen als Reduktion von Komplexität," in: *Neusprachliche Mitteilungen* 2, 88-94.

Krzeszowski, Tomasz P. 1971. "Equivalence, congruence and deep structure," in: G. Nickel (ed.), *Papers in Contrastive Linguistics*, Stuttgart, 37-48.

Kromann, Hans-Peder, T. Riiber and P. Rosbach. 1984. "'Active' and 'passive' bilingual dictionaries: The Ščerba concept reconsidered," in: R.R.K. Hartmann (ed.), *LEXeter '83 Proceedings*, Tübingen: Niemeyer, 207-215.

Kurth, Ernst-Norbert. 1995. *Metaphernübersetzung. Dargestellt an grotesken Metaphern im Früwerk Charles Dickens in der Wiedergabe deutscher Übersetzungen*, Frankfurt: Lang.

Kussmaul, Paul. 1986. "Übersetzen als Entscheidungsprozeß. Die Rolle der Fehleranalyse in der Übersetzungsdidaktik," in: M. Snell-Hornby (ed.), *Übersetzungswissenschaft — Eine Neuorientierung*, 206-229.

Lakoff, George. 1970. *Irregularity in Syntax*, New York: Holt.

-----. 1977. "Linguistic Gestalts," in: *Proceedings of the Thirteenth Regional Meeting of the Chicago Linguistic Society*, Chicago, 236-287.

-----. 1982. *Categories and Cognitive Models*, Trier: LAUT.

Lakoff, George and Mark Johnson. 1980. *Metaphors We Live By*, Chicago: University of Chicago Press.

Lambert, José, Lieven D'hulst and Katrin van Bragt. 1985. "Translated Literature in France, 1800-1850," in: T. Hermans (ed.), *The Manipulation of Literature*, 149-163.

Landsberger, Benno. 1974. "Die Eigenbegrifflichkeit der babylonischen Welt" (rpt. Islamica II. 1926), Darmstadt: Wiss. Buchgesellschaft, 1-18.

Lange, Hartmut. 1984. "Begegnung zwischen Praxis und Lehre. Ein BDÜ-Symposium," in: *Mitteilungsblatt für Dolmetscher und Übersetzer* 1, 1-2.

Langhoff, Stephan. 1980. *Gestaltlinguistik. Eine ganzheitliche Beschreibung syntaktisch-semantischer Sprachfunktionen am Beispiel modaler Infinitivkonstruktionen des Deutschen und Englischen*, Frankfurt: Lang.

Leech, Geoffrey N. 1969. *A Linguistic Guide to English Poetry*, London: Longman.

-----. 1974. *Semantics*, Harmondsworth: Penguin.

Leech, Geoffrey N. and Michael H. Short. 1981. *Style in fiction. A linguistic introduction to English fictional prose*, London: Longman.

Lefevere, André. 1984. "Teaching Literary Translation: The Possible and the Impossible," in: W. Wilss and G. Thome (eds.), *Translation Theory and its Implementation in the Teaching of Translating and Interpreting*, Tübingen: Narr, 90-97.

Leisi, Ernst. 1973. *Praxis der englischen Semantik*, Heidelberg: Winter.

-----. 1975. *Der Wortinhalt. Seine Struktur im Deutschen und Englischen*, Heidelberg: Quelle & Meyer.

Levý, Jiří. 1967. "Translation as a Decision Process," in: *To Honor Roman Jakobson. Essays on the Occasion of his 70th Birthday*, The Hague: Mouton, 1171-1182.

-----. 1969. *Die literarischen Übersetzung. Theorie einer Kunstgattung* (tr. from Czech *Umění překladu*, 1963, by Walter Schamschula), Frankfurt: Athenäum.

Lodge, David. 1966. *Language of Fiction. Essays in Criticism and Verbal Analysis of the English Novel*, London: Routledge and Kegan Paul.

Lyons, John. 1968. *Introduction to Theoretical Linguistics*, Cambridge: Cambridge University Press.

Merz, Dagmar. 1986. *Die Perspektive als Translationsproblem bei politischen Reden — dargestellt an ausgewählten Textbeispielen*, Diploma thesis, unpubl. ms., Heidelberg.

Milic, Louis T. 1967. *A Quantitative Approach to the Style of Jonathan Swift*, The Hague: Mouton.

Moser-Mercer, Barbara. 1986. "Schnittstelle Mensch/Maschine: Interaktion oder Konfrontation?," in: M. Snell-Hornby (ed.), *Übersetzungswissenschaft — Eine Neuorientierung*, 311-330.

Mounin, Georges. 1967. *Die Übersetzung. Geschichte, Theorie, Anwendung* (tr. from Italian *Teoria e Storia della Traduzione* by Harro Stammerjohann), München: Nymphenburg.

Neubert, Albrecht. 1984. "Text-bound Translation Teaching," in: W. Wilss and G. Thome (eds.), *Translation Theory and its Implementation in the Teaching of Translating and Interpreting*, Tübingen: Narr, 61-70.

-----. 1986. "Translatorische Relativität," in: M. Snell-Hornby (ed.), *Übersetzungswissenschaft — Eine Neuorientierung*, 85-105.

-----. 1986a. "Dichtung und Wahrheit des zweisprachigen Wörterbuchs," in: *Sitzungsberichte der Sächsischen Akademie der Wissenschaften zu Leipzig*, Vol.126, 4, 1-23.

Newmark, Peter. 1981. *Approaches To Translation*, Oxford: Pergamon.

-----. 1985. "The Translation of Metaphor," in: W. Paprotté and R. Dirven (eds.), *The Ubiquity of Metaphor*, Amsterdam: Benjamins, 295-326.

Nida, Eugene A. 1964. *Toward a Science of Translating. With special reference to principles and procedures involved in Bible translating*, Leiden: Brill.

Nida, Eugene A. and Charles R. Taber. 1969. *The Theory and Practice of Translation*, Leiden: Brill.

Nord, Christiane. 1991. *Text Analysis in Translation. Theory, Methodology, and Didactic Application of a Model for Translation-oriented Text Analysis*. (tr. from German *Textanalyse und Übersetzen* by Christiane Nord and Penelope Sparrow), Amsterdam: Rodopi.

O'Donnell, W.R. and Loreto Todd. 1980. *Variety in Contemporary English*, London: Allen & Unwin.

Ogden, Charles Kay and Ivor Armstrong Richards. 1969. *The Meaning of Meaning*, London: Routledge.

Oittinen, Riitta. 1993. *I am Me — I am Other. On the Dialogics of Translating for Children*, Tampere: Univ. Press.

Oksaar, Els. 1988. *Kulturemtheorie. Ein Beitrag zur Sprachverwendungsforschung*. Göttingen: Vandenhoeck.

Paepcke, Fritz. 1978. "Übersetzen als hermeneutischer Entwurf," in: *Savonlinnan Kieli-Instituutti 1968-1978*, Savonlinnassa, 47-67.

-----. 1980. "Textverstehen und Übersetzen," in: *Babel* 4, 199-204.

-----. 1981. "Übersetzen zwischen Regel und Spiel," in: *Mitteilungsblatt für Dolmetscher und Übersetzer* 1, 1-13.

-----. 1985. "Textverstehen — Textübersetzen — Übersetzungskritik," in: *Mitteilungsblatt für Dolmetscher und Übersetzer* 3, 1-11.

Paepcke, Fritz und Philippe Forget. 1981. *Textverstehen und Übersetzen/ Ouvertures sur la traduction*, Heidelberg: Groos.

Paulovsky, Louis H. 1983. "Prinzipien der akademischen Übersetzer- und Dolmetscherausbildung an der Universität Wien," in: *Festschrift zum 40-jährigen Bestehen des Instituts für Übersetzer- und Dolmetscherausbildung der Universität Wien*, Wien: Ott, 140-146.

Popovič, Anton. 1984. "From J. Levý to Communicational Didactics of Literary Translation," in: W. Wilss and G. Thome (eds.), *Translation Theory and its Implementation in the Teaching of Translating and Interpreting*, Tübingen: Narr, 98-104.

Popp, Klaus-Jürgen. 1976. "Elisabeth Schnack und Carson McCullers: Die Ballade vom traurigen Übersetzen," in: H.W. Drescher und S. Scheffzek (eds.), *Theorie und Praxis des Übersetzens und Dolmetschens*, Bern: Lang, 107-123.

Quine, Willard Van Orman. 1960. *Word and Object*, Cambridge: MIT Press.

Quirk, Randolph, Sidney Greenbaum, Geoffrey Leech and Jan Svartvik. 1972. *A Grammar of Contemporary English*, London: Longman.

Quirk, Randolph and Sidney Greenbaum. 1973. *A University Grammar of English*, London: Longman.

Reich-Ranicki, Marcel. 1982. "Der Dolchstoß des Übersetzers," in: *Frankfurter Allgemeine Zeitung*, 4.12.1982.

Reiss, Katharina. 1971. *Möglichkeiten und Grenzen der Übersetzungskritik. Kategorien und Kriterien für eine sachgerechte Beurteilung von Übersetzungen*, München: Hueber.

-----. 1976. *Texttyp und Übersetzungsmethode. Der operative Text*, Kronberg: Scriptor.

-----. 1982. "Zur Übersetzung von Kinder- und Jugendbüchern. Theorie und Praxis," in: *Lebende Sprachen* 1, 7-13.

-----. 1984. "Methodische Fragen der übersetzungsrelevanten Textanalyse. Die Reichweite der Laswell-Formel," in: *Lebende Sprachen* 1, 7-9.

Reiss, Katharina and Hans J. Vermeer. 1984. *Grundlegung einer allgemeinen Translationstheorie*, Tübingen: Niemeyer.

Rose, Marilyn Gaddis. 1981. "Translation Types and Conventions," in: M.G. Rose (ed.), *Translation Spectrum. Essays in Theory and Practice*, Albany: New York Press, 31-40.

Ross, Stephen. 1981. "Translation and Similarity," in: M.G. Rose (ed.), *Translation Spectrum. Essays in Theory and Practice*, Albany: New York Press, 8-22.

Rosch, Eleanor. 1973. "Natural categories," in: *Cognitive Psychology* 4, 328-350.

Scherner, Manfred. 1984. *Sprache als Text. Ansätze zu einer sprachwissenschaftlich begründeten Theorie des Textverstehens. Forschungsgeschichte — Problemstellung — Beschreibung*, Tübingen: Niemeyer.

Schmid, Annemarie. 1986. "Übersetzungsausbildung und Übersetzeralltag," in: M. Snell-Hornby (ed.), *Übersetzungswissenschaft — Eine Neuorientierung*, 375-390.

Schmitt, Peter A. 1986. "Die 'Eindeutigkeit' von Fachtexten: Bemerkungen zu einer Fiktion," in: M. Snell-Hornby (ed.), *Übersetzungswissenschaft — Eine Neuorientierung*, 252-282.

Schultze, Brigitte. 1986. "Theorie der Dramenübersetzung — 1960 bis heute. Ein Bericht zur Forschungslage," unpubl. ms.

Schultze, Brigitte et al. 1990. *Literatur und Theater. Traditionen und Konventionen als Problem der Dramenübersetzung*, Tübingen: Narr.

Searle, John R. 1969. *Speech acts: An essay in the philosophy of language*, Cambridge: Cambridge University Press.

Senn, Fritz. 1986. "Literarische Übertragungen — empirisches Bedenken," in: M. Snell-Hornby, *Übersetzungswissenschaft — Eine Neuorientierung*, 54-84.

Shibles, Warren A. 1970. *Metaphor: An Annotated Bibliography and History*, Wisconsin: Language Press.

Snell-Hornby, Mary. 1983. *Verb-descriptivity in German and English. A contrastive study in semantic fields*, Heidelberg: Winter.

-----. 1984. "Sprechbare Sprache — Spielbarer Text. Zur Problematik der Bühnenübersetzung," in: R. Watts and U. Weidmann (eds.), *Modes of Interpretation. Essays Presented to Ernst Leisi*, Tübingen: Narr, 101-116.

-----. 1984a. "Dimension and perspective in literary translation," in: W. Wilss and G. Thome (eds.), *Translation Theory and its Implementation in the Teaching of Translating and Interpreting*, Tübingen: Narr, 105-113.

-----. 1984b. *Statements, Questions and Directives*, Trier: LAUT.

-----. 1984c. "The linguistic structure of public directives in German and English," in: *Multilingua* 4, 203-211.

-----. 1985. "Übersetzungswissenschaft und Anglistik," in: M. Pfister (ed.), *Anglistentag 1984, Passau. Vorträge*, Giessen: Hoffmann, 411-423.

-----. (ed.) 1986. *Übersetzungswissenschaft — Eine Neuorientierung. Zur Integrierung von Theorie und Praxis*, Tübingen: Francke.

-----. 1986a. "Übersetzen, Sprache, Kultur," in: M. Snell-Hornby (ed.), *Übersetzungswissenschaft — Eine Neuorientierung*, 9-29.

-----. 1986b. "The bilingual dictionary — Victim of its own tradition?," in: R.R.K. Hartmann (ed.), *The History of Lexicography*, Amsterdam: Benjamins, 207-218.

-----. 1988. "The unfamiliar image. Metaphor as a problem in translation," in: H.W. Ludwig (ed.), *Anglistentag 1987*. Tübingen. Vorträge, Giessen: Hoffmann, 258-269.

-----. 1992. "The professional translator of tomorrow: language specialist or all-round expert?", in: C. Dollerup and A. Loddegaard (eds.), *Teaching Translation and Interpreting. Training, Talent and Experience*, Amsterdam: Benjamins.

Snell-Hornby, Mary, Franz Pöchhacker and Klaus Kaindl (eds.). 1994. *Translation Studies. An Interdiscipline*, Amsterdam: Benjamins.

Sprengel, Konrad. 1979. "Cinderella, or: English language courses at German universities," in: M. van de Velde and W. Vandeweghe (eds.), *Sprachstruktur, Individuum und Gesellschaft*, Vol.1, Tübingen: Niemeyer, 349-358.

Stein, Dieter. 1980. *Theoretische Grundlagen der Übersetzungswissenschaft*, Tübingen: Narr.

Steiner, George. 1975. *After Babel. Aspects of Language and Translation*, London: Oxford University Press.

Stellbrink, Hans-Jürgen. 1984. "Der Übersetzer in der Industrie: Beschäftigungsaussichten und Verdienstmöglichkeiten," Guest Lecture Saarbrücken 30.5.1984, unpubl. ms.

-----. 1984a. "Die Aufgaben eines Fremdsprachendienstes beim Abschluß von fremdsprachigen Verträgen," Guest Lecture Hildesheim 12.11.1984, unpubl. ms.

-----. 1985. "Die Tätigkeit des Dolmetschers und Übersetzers in der Industrie: Meistens nicht wie im Lehrbuch," Guest Lecture Heidelberg 1.2.1985, unpubl. ms.

Stolze, Radegundis. 1982. *Grundlagen der Textübersetzung*, Heidelberg: Groos.

-----. 1984. "Übersetzen, was dasteht? Die Übersetzung im Spannungsfeld von Textlinguistik und Hermeneutik," in: *Mitteilungsblatt für Dolmetscher und Übersetzer* 6, 1-8.

-----. 1986. "Zur Bedeutung von Hermeneutik und Textlinguistik beim Übersetzen," in: M. Snell-Hornby (ed.), *Übersetzungswissenschaft — Eine Neuorientierung*, 133-159.

-----. 1988. "Das begriffliche Bedeutungspotential als Problem der Lexikographie," in: M. Snell-Hornby (ed.), *ZüriLEX '86 Proceedings*, Tübingen: Francke, 27-35.

Störig, Hans J. (ed.). 1973. *Das Problem des Übersetzens*, Darmstadt: Wiss. Buchgesellschaft.

Thiel, Gisela. 1981. "Überlegungen zur übersetzungsrelevanten Textanalyse," in: W. Wilss (ed.), *Übersetzungswissenschaft*, Darmstadt: Wiss. Buchgesellschaft, 367-384.

Toury, Gideon. 1980. *In Search of a Theory of Translation*, Tel-Aviv: Porter Institute.

-----. 1980a. "The Translator as a Nonconformist-to-be, or: How to Train Translators So As to Violate Translational Norms," in: S.-O. Poulsen and W. Wilss (eds.), *Angewandte Übersetzungswissenschaft. Internationales übersetzungswissenschaftliches Kolloquium an der Wirtschaftsuniversität Ärhus, Dänemark*, Ärhus, 180-194.

-----. 1984. "The Notion of 'Native Translator' and Translation Teaching," in: W. Wilss and G. Thome (eds.), *Translation Theory and its Implementation in the Teaching of Translating and Interpreting*, Tübingen: Narr, 105-113.

-----. 1986. "Translating English Literature via German — and vice versa. A Symptomatic Reversal in the History of Modern Hebrew Literature," Paper read at the International Symposium of the Sonderforschungsbereich 309 "Die Literarische Übersetzung," Göttingen, October 1986, unpubl. ms.

Tytler, Alexander Fraser, Lord Woodhouselee. 1978. *Essay on the Principles of Translation*, ed. J.F. Huntsman, Amsterdam: Benjamins.

Ullmann, Stephen. 1973. *Meaning and Style*, Oxford: Blackwell.

Vachek, Josef. 1966. *The Linguistic School of Prague. An Introduction to its Theory and Practice*, Bloomington: Indiana University Press.

Vanderauwera, Ria. 1985. "The Response to Translated Literature. A Sad Example," in: T. Hermans (ed.), *The Manipulation of Literature*, 198-214.

Vannerem, Mia and Mary Snell-Hornby. 1986. "Die Szene hinter dem Text: 'scenes-and-frames semantics' in der Übersetzung," in: M. Snell-Hornby (ed.), *Übersetzungswissenschaft — Eine Neurorientierung*, 184-205.

Van den Broeck, Raymond. 1981. "The limits of translatability exemplified by metaphor translation," in: *Poetics Today* 4, 73-87.

Van Gorp, Hendrik. 1985. "Translation and Literary Genre. The European Picaresque Novel in the 17th and 18th Centuries," in: T. Hermans (ed.), *The Manipulation of Literature*, 136-148.

Van Noppen, J.P., S. de Knop, R. Jongen. 1985. *Metaphor. A Bibliography of post-1970 publications*, Amsterdam: Benjamins.

Verch, Maria. 1976. "Zum Problem englisch-deutscher Übersetzungen von Jugendliteratur," in: *Revue d'Allemagne* VIII, 3, 466-473.

Vermeer, Hans J. 1971. *Einführung in die linguistische Terminologie*, München: Nymphenburg.

-----. 1983. *Aufsätze zur Translationstheorie*, Heidelberg, mimeo.

-----. 1986. "Übersetzen als kultureller Transfer," in: M. Snell-Hornby (ed.), *Übersetzungswissenschaft — Eine Neuorientierung*, 30-53.

Vermeer, Hans J. and Heidrun Witte. 1990. *Mögen Sie Zistrosen? Scenes & frames & channels im translatorischen Handeln*, TextConText Beiheft 3. Heidelberg: Groos.

Vinay, J.-P. and J. Darbelnet. 1958. *Stylistique Comparée du Français et de l'Anglais. Méthode de traduction*, Paris: Didier.

Wandruszka, Mario. 1969. *Sprachen, vergleichbar und unvergleichlich*, München: Piper.

-----. 1971. *Interlinguistik. Umrisse einer neuen Sprachwissenschaft*, München: Piper.

-----. 1979. *Die Mehrsprachligkeit des Menschen*, München: Piper.

-----. 1985. "Der Übersetzer und seine Stellung in der Öffentlichkeit," in: H. Bühler (ed.), *X. Weltkongreß der FIT. Kongreßakte*, Wien: Braumüller, 55-64.

Weaver, W. 1955. "Translation, a memorandum," in: W.N. Locke and A.D. Booth (eds.), *Machine Translation of Languages*, New York: Wiley, 15-23.

Weinreich, Uriel. 1966. "Explorations in semantic theory," in: T.A. Sebeok (ed.), *Current Trends in Linguistics* 3, The Hague: Mouton, 395-477.

Weinrich, Harald. 1976. *Sprache in Texten*, Stuttgart: Klett.

Wertheimer, Max. 1912/1959. *Productive Thinking*, Chicago: Chicago University Press.

Whorf, Benjamin L. 1973. *Language, thought and reality. Selected writings*, ed. J.B. Carroll, Cambridge: MIT Press.

Wilss, Wolfram. 1977. *Übersetzungswissenschaft. Probleme und Methoden*, Stuttgart: Klett.

-----. 1977a. "Textanalyse und Übersetzen," in: K.-H. Bender, K. Berger and M. Wandruszka (eds.), *Imago Linguae. Beiträge zu Sprache, Deutung und Übersetzen. Festschrift zum 60. Geburtstag von Fritz Paepcke*, München: Fink, 625-653.

-----. 1980. "Semiotik und Übersetzungswissenschaft," in: W. Wilss (ed.), *Semiotik und Übersetzen*, Tübingen: Narr.

-----. 1985. "Theorie und Praxis des Übersetzens," in: H. Bühler (ed.), *X. Weltkongreß der FIT. Kongreßakte*, Wien: Braumüller, 315-320.

-----. 1987. "Handlungstheoretische und verhaltenswissenschaftliche Aspekte der Übersetzungswissenschaft," unpubl. ms.

Winter, Helmut. 1981. "Die Schokoladentorte zwickt an mir," in: *Frankfurter Allgemeine Zeitung*, 16.10.1981.

Wittgenstein, Ludwig. 1953. *Philosophical Investigations*, Oxford: Blackwell.

Zgusta, Ladislav. 1984. "Translational equivalence in the bilingual dictionary," in: R.R.K. Hartmann (ed.), *LEXeter '83 Proceedings*, Tübingen: Niemeyer, 147-154.

Index of Names

This index is not exhaustive and aims primarily at clarity of presentation. Authors discussed in the text are listed here, whereas references are not.

Index of Key Terms